MW00649011

557 MARIBELLA COURT
NEW SMYRNA BEACH, FL 32168

LEMISH

PRAISE FOR *A GRAND SLAM FOR GOD*

"Every kid has athletic aspirations—dreams of being the one that helps their team win it all. Fr. Burke Masters describes in *A Grand Slam for God* how he got that moment in college. As you discover through Fr. Burke's life story, Christ revealed to him that while those particular moments are great, they are not the eternal reward our hearts desire. Through the grace of many other 'grand slam' moments in his life—from a religious sister giving him homework to read the Gospel of Matthew, to finding a deep love for the Eucharist after accidentally receiving his First Communion, to unthinkable family tragedy, to the miraculous healing of a little girl, and finally culminating to a full circle moment in 2016—Fr. Burke's life shows us that certain people enter our lives and certain events can happen that point us back to our eternal reward, our eternal grand slam."

—Trevor Williams, MLB pitcher, Washington Nationals

"*A Grand Slam for God* is a highly inspiring and encouraging story that will evoke much pondering in your own life. Through honesty, engaging witness, and vulnerability, Fr. Burke reveals that God honors and authors the deepest desires of our heart. In both sorrow and triumph, all things work for good according to his will. You will love this book!"

—Sr. Miriam James Heidland, SOLT, speaker and author

"Every priest has a vocation story, a story of God's grace and a man's cooperation with that grace. As Bishop of Joliet, I had the privilege of ministering with Fr. Burke for four years. I got to know him well, but not until reading *A Grand Slam for God* did I learn the full interior history of his vocation to the priesthood. Surprised by God at every turn, Fr. Burke listened deeply to the interior movements of the Holy Spirit and joyfully accepted God's call to the priesthood. This book will be an inspiration to young men considering a priestly vocation—but it will also be a reminder for all of us to discover anew the grace that accompanies God's call in each of our lives. It is a reminder to give thanks for the blessings God showers down upon us."

—Archbishop J. Peter Sartain, Archbishop Emeritus of Seattle

"Fr. Burke is a calm listener who is there for everyone and always available. He is an old-school priest and friend, a trusted member within the clubhouse, and a pretty good ballplayer too. You will enjoy this book about his amazing life story."

—Joe Maddon, former MLB manager and coauthor of *The Book of Joe*

"Early on in my friendship with Fr. Burke, I had the opportunity to witness a conversation between him and Mike Martin, the winningest coach in college baseball history. They reminisced about that electrifying moment for Burke (his grand slam) and the agonizing effect for Coach Martin when his team was knocked out of the World Series. By the end of the conversation, they were both speaking joyfully about their fulfillment in their faith in Jesus Christ. I trust you will love reading this inspiring story of a man who hungered for greatness and was surprised where he found it."

—Dr. Bob Schuchts, author of *Be Healed*

"This book has it all: a captivating tale of a hometown boy who makes it big, but not at all in the way he expected. The true story of Fr. Burke Masters' unexpected and amazing trajectory from high school star athlete to college baseball superstar to the Catholic priesthood is filled with natural-born talent, hard work, true grit, determination, and trust in God's loving providence, with plenty of triumphs, surprises, and unexpected bumps in the road along the way. I loved it."

—Patrick Madrid, host of the daily *Patrick Madrid Show* on Relevant Radio

"I encourage anyone and everyone that likes baseball to read this incredible book written by Fr. Burke. He uses his own experiences with failure and success in the great sport of baseball to teach us about who we are and who God is. This book will give us the hope, courage, and inspiration to be all that God has created us to be. A definite must read!"

—Deacon Darrell Miller, former California Angels baseball player (1979–1989)

"Fr. Burke Masters' autobiography *A Grand Slam for God* is the detailed journey of his conversion from seeking his will to seeking God's will. He beautifully tells the story of how a college baseball star gave up the tools of the game in order to labor in the Lord's vineyard as a priest. It is truly an inspired tale for everyone, as at the heart of this story we hear one man's account of radically falling in love with Jesus Christ. Enjoy!"

—Bishop James S. Wall, Diocese of Gallup

"Few subjects are of more compelling interest than sport and religion. The narrative to which we are introduced in *A Grand Slam for God* involves both of them. It's a story so fresh, so bold and disarmingly honest, it captures and holds the reader's attention from first page to last. Not only is it a great read, it's also an instructive pointer to what St. John Paul II referred to once, when speaking to a group of highly successful sportsmen and athletes, as 'that final target, that "goal" which is the true and ultimate destiny of life.'"

—Fr. Paul Murray, OP, author and international speaker

A GRAND SLAM FOR GOD

FOREWORD BY MIKE SWEENEY FR. BURKE MASTERS

A GRAND SLAM FOR GOD

A JOURNEY
FROM
BASEBALL
STAR TO
CATHOLIC
PRIEST

WORD on FIRE.

Published by Word on Fire,
Elk Grove Village, IL 60007
© 2023 by Burke Masters
Printed in the United States of America
All rights reserved

Cover design, typesetting, and interior art direction by Nicolas Fredrickson, Clark Kenyon, and Rozann Lee. Cover photo courtesy of the Knights of Columbus and Spirit Juice Studios.

Scripture excerpts are from the New Revised Standard Version Bible: Catholic Edition (copyright © 1989, 1993), used by permission of the National Council of the Churches of Christ in the United States of America. All rights reserved worldwide.

First printing, August 2023

ISBN: 978-1-68578-993-0

Library of Congress Control Number: 2022943338

CONTENTS

Foreword: Mike Sweeney   ix

Preface   xiii

Acknowledgments   xv

Chapter One: A Perfect Game Plan   1

Chapter Two: Meeting Jesus   13

Chapter Three: A Change of Plans   25

Chapter Four: A Divided Heart   41

Chapter Five: The Gift of the Red Bird   55

Chapter Six: Father What-a-Waste!   72

Chapter Seven: A Friend of Jesús   84

Chapter Eight: Living in the Moment   94

Chapter Nine: Searching for My Identity   103

Chapter Ten: A Grand Slam for God   120

Questions for Reflection and Discussion   134

FOREWORD

Mike Sweeney

I will never forget the evening of June 17, 1994. I was a twenty-one-year-old catcher from Southern California playing Minor League Baseball for the Rockford Royals, a Single-A affiliate of the Kansas City Royals. I was having the best season of my young career, hitting well over .300 while helping lead my team to a league-leading record. It was a typical hot and humid Midwest day, and my teammates and I were preparing to play a Friday night road game against the Kane County Cougars, a Single-A affiliate of the Miami Marlins, in Geneva, Illinois. Although we were a short drive from the "MLB Cathedrals" Wrigley Field (Chicago Cubs) and Comiskey Park (Chicago White Sox), we felt like we were millions of miles away from living out our big league dreams. Although the odds of Minor League players making it to the big leagues are slim, the fans in attendance were about to watch a staggering twenty-one future Major League players that evening. What an atmosphere the spectators were able to take in for about a $3 ticket stub.

Minor League Baseball is an absolute grind and could be accurately described as Major League Purgatory. The twelve-hour workdays at dilapidated Minor League stadiums were long and arduous. The 140 games in just 150 calendar days while staying at roach-infested, dumpy motels were unrelenting. Ten-hour bus trips in a rectangular forty-foot salvage yard steel box on wheels filled with the stench of thirty athletes, greasy fast-food leftovers, and chain-smoking, coffee-drinking bus drivers were simply part of the job. On road trips, a tall cup of black coffee and a donut served as payment for the driver to take me and my Catholic teammates to Sunday Mass in the bus. To get to and from our home stadium in Rockford, two teammates and I pitched in $100 each to purchase a 1978 Pontiac Grand Safari wagon—a mustard-colored, wood-paneled eyesore nicknamed "The Hoopty." Since we didn't have enough money for registration, we took a black sharpie and changed the expiration month on the temporary document from 04/30/1994 to "09"/30/1994 to cover the season. Sorry Lord: this was Minor League Baseball, and I was simply trying to survive! These were the best and yet the worst times of my life.

Back to that muggy night game in June. In the top of the sixth inning, with the score knotted up at 3–3, the atmosphere grew tense and dark when the lights around the stadium suddenly turned off. A faulty transformer had blown a fuse, and a backup generator only powered some emergency lighting and televisions in the luxury suites. After about thirty minutes, I found myself down the third-base line talking with two young boys sporting Little League uniforms who begged for baseballs from our team ballbag. I promised them that if they came back with two hot dogs, they would each get an official autographed team baseball. The exchange left both of us feeling like winners. As I sat in the bullpen eating ballpark "filet mignon" on a bun, my attention was drawn to the illuminated suite directly behind home plate. With the stadium so dark, its large television shined like the North Star, and I saw a silhouette of one of the Kane County managers frantically pacing back and forth in front of the TV. Curious about what was causing the stir, I walked up into our clubhouse, where all my teammates were glued to the television. They briefed me that the scene before our eyes—a white 1993 Ford Bronco with O.J. Simpson in a slow-speed chase with the LAPD on a California freeway—was being seen on almost every TV in the country. Eventually, the lights of the stadium came back to life, and the game ended close to midnight due to the delays. It was just another crazy night of Minor League Baseball on the journey of making my big league dreams a reality.

Almost twenty years later, as a recently retired five-time MLB All-Star, I was attending a Catholic Athletes for Christ (CAC) men's retreat in Malibu, California. CAC is a ministry that brings the Gospel of Jesus Christ and his Holy Catholic Church to the world through athletics. They host retreats and camps, help to provide Mass every Sunday during the NFL and MLB seasons, and empower Catholic athletes ("Cathletes") around the world to become the saints that God has called them to be. While on this life-changing retreat with Hall of Famers Mike Piazza, Vin Scully, Vince Coleman, and Trevor Hoffman, I was blessed to hear a Catholic priest named Fr. Burke Masters, known as "The Baseball Priest," share his testimony. This handsome priest, the vocation director in Joliet, IL, embodied St. Francis of Assisi's gentleness, St. Paul's zeal, and St. Dominic's desire to set the world on fire for Jesus. After hearing him speak, most of the men in attendance were moved to tears, and many were ready to join the seminary. When the standing ovation ended, I introduced myself to this humble man of God, and after about five minutes, I realized that I would have a friend in him for the rest of my life. While in conversation, I smiled in disbelief when he mentioned working in management in 1994 with the Kane County Cougars. We almost fell over laughing when we realized that I was the player down the third-base line exchanging hot dogs for baseballs and he was the one pacing frantically in the luxury suite behind home plate on that crazy night when the lights went out in Geneva.

Little did I know then that this Minor League manager pacing in his team's suite had an amazing story and big league dreams of his own. He was already a local celebrity due to his athletic greatness, humble demeanor, leadership ability, and strong family name. As a gifted and highly touted star athlete at one of the Joliet parochial high schools, he was on the fast track to greatness. He was a blue chip recruit out of high school and a four-year starter at an SEC powerhouse university, and he played professionally with a Chicago White Sox affiliate. After his dreams of playing in the MLB came to an end, he had ambitions of making it as a general manager. Besides being an incredible athlete, he was a number-crunching, mathematical genius on track to be a "Moneyball" type of leader. Around this time, he was also falling in love with God. This love grew to a point where he gave up everything, including his baseball dreams, to honor it, becoming a consecrated soldier for the Church as a priest. Despite never playing in the Major Leagues, his story is more powerful than that of any member of the Hall of Fame in Cooperstown.

Since meeting Fr. Burke almost ten years ago, he has become a brother, a best friend, and even the godfather of our sixth child, who was named after this heroic priest that my family and I love. The home run–hitting slugger from Joliet, IL, has become a power hitter for Christ. He has replaced his baseball uniform with a black cassock and a Roman collar, his bat with a rosary, and his briefcase with a Mass kit.

The story you're about to read is similar to the one I heard the night I met Fr. Burke Masters at the retreat in California. I think you'll agree that he has truly hit a "Grand Slam for God."

PREFACE

I had the incredible opportunity to walk the Camino de Santiago de Compostela in Spain from April 14 to May 17, 2022, with my friends Rick, Ed, Joe, Mark, Tom, Mike, and Mike. We tallied 1.2 million steps over the thirty-four days of walking. It was one of the most exhilarating, challenging, and life-changing experiences of my life.

We started in Saint-Jean-Pied-de-Port, France. We averaged just over fifteen miles per day. Along the way, we would pray, converse with strangers, talk with each other, and at times walk in silence.

It was interesting how the Camino transformed us. The first two weeks, we were focused on getting to the next town. Little by little, we began to enjoy the scenery and the people along the way. The goal came to be less about the destination and more about the journey. We began to enjoy the people and the scenery much more.

Life is like the Camino. Hopefully we learn that it's not just about getting to the next destination, but it's about the journey. This book is about my journey through life. My life did not turn out like I thought it would. I thank God that his plans for me were different than mine. Hopefully reading about my story will help you reflect on your Camino of life. Enjoy the journey. *Buen Camino!*

ACKNOWLEDGMENTS

I would like to first thank God for creating me, sustaining me, and loving me. I am grateful for all the experiences of my life, even the ones that I didn't appreciate when they were happening to me.
I thank my parents, Tod and Janet, for their love and encouragement. They made me believe that anything is possible if I put my mind to it. I also thank my brothers, Brock and Blaine, for their constant and abiding friendship. Thank you to my niece Mackenzie, who helped me get this project from my mind onto paper.

Thank you to all who have shaped me with your amazing love and support over the years. I feel so blessed with the most incredible family and friends. There are so many of you that I am afraid to leave someone out if I tried to list you all.

Thank you to Bert Ghezzi and Joe Durepos, who believed in me and in this book enough to see it to publication.

Finally, I would like to place this book under the patronage of St. John Vianney, the patron saint of priests, whose story has always inspired me.

CHAPTER ONE

A PERFECT GAME PLAN

The highlight of my baseball career at Mississippi State occurred on May 26, 1990, at a game during the regional tournament to qualify for the College World Series in Omaha, Nebraska. And that special experience would be life changing for me.

I was in the zone, which means that the game slows down to the point that you feel like you are in total control. In that tournament, I was in the zone more than ever before in my athletic career. Our first game was against Brigham Young. I had four hits in five at bats, and we won 16–5. The next night we played the University of Illinois. Highly motivated playing against a home state team, I went two for three. We won the game 5–3. That victory put us in the winner's bracket in the double-elimination tournament.

In the next game we played a Florida State team that was ranked first or second in the nation most of the year. My grandparents and my brother Blaine and his wife were in the stands. My confidence level was at a high that I'd never experienced. The first five times up to bat I got base hits. The baseball looked like a balloon in slow motion. It was saying "Here! Hit me!"

I came up in the top of the ninth inning, down by a run with the bases loaded. The stadium buzzed with anticipation. Florida State had their best pitcher on the mound, there was one out, and I worked the count to three and one. In the box I thought, "Take a pitch; if he walks you, the game is tied."

"What are you doing?" my inner voice retorted. I was seeing the ball so well. I took my time, stepped out of the box, and had this internal conversation. "If he throws you a strike, just swing at it; you're on fire." So that's what I did. With the count at three and one, he had to throw a strike. He threw a fastball—probably 93 mph—but it looked like it was moving in slow motion. I simply reacted and swung the bat effortlessly, and the ball jumped off the bat so perfectly that I didn't even feel it.

In the past, whenever I hit a home run, the ball would barely clear the fence. I'd take off running, thinking it would just be a double. But as soon as I hit this one, I knew that it was gone. It cleared the first two rows of pick-up trucks in the famous lot nicknamed the "Left Field Lounge." The left fielder took a step, stopped, and slumped his head into his chest. I dropped the bat and looked at my teammates in the first base dugout. They all raised their hands in excitement. The whole stadium exploded. "A grand slam for Masters! A grand slam for Masters!" Jim Ellis, our play-by-play radio announcer, exclaimed. "This crowd is berserk!"[*]

I never showed emotion when I was playing because Dad taught us to play on an even keel. He said, "If I show up in the last inning, I better not be able to tell from your face if you are zero-for-four or four-for-four. You better not be pouting, or you better not be too high." So that's how I always played, even though I felt a thrill of excitement deep down. But this time, as I ran the bases, I couldn't hold it in. I raised my arms up in the air as I was rounding third base and all my teammates were jumping up and down at home plate. The roar of the crowd was deafening. I will never forget that moment as long as I live. I knew something special had just happened.

[*] You can watch Burke's life-changing home run on YouTube. Search for "Burke Masters grand slam."

We still had to hold them for three more outs to win the game, as we were the visitors for this tournament game even though we were playing at home. I recorded all three assists in the bottom of the ninth inning with a level of adrenaline I seldom experienced. After the final out, my brother Blaine jumped the fence and celebrated with us on the pitcher's mound. We had not yet won the tournament, but we were in the driver's seat.

The grand slam sealed my decision to live baseball and make it my career. I believed I was on my way to the Major Leagues—a perfect game plan. Little did I know that I was really on my way to becoming the Baseball Priest.

* * *

Being athletic was an important value in our family. Both my parents had been athletes, and sports were in our blood. Even as kids, my older brothers Brock and Blaine were good athletes. But I was clumsy and uncoordinated and not very good at any game. It seemed that I couldn't walk across the street without falling over myself. Dad once told Mom, while watching me run, "It's a good thing the other two are athletes because God knows Burke will never be one."

Awkward as I was, I still tried to keep pace with Brock and Blaine. And what they called "character building" I called "torture." We fought, and when we fought, we fought hard. Did they go easy on me because I was the smallest kid in our family and on our block? No, they did not. Brock was older by seven years and Blaine by almost three, and there was no playing the youngest card with them. It was either keep up or sit out, and I was not about to sit out. I had inherited a strong Masters' trait: stubbornness. When I complained to my parents, they reminded me, "If you want to play with them, you either play by their rules or you don't play at all." So I decided to play, and I struggled to improve and match their skills. It was not easy though. My temper

3

and my clumsiness only spurred my brothers to tease me even more. It felt like their favorite pastime was to get me riled up.

During the winters in our first house, Dad would build an ice rink for us in the backyard. He nailed two-by-sixes together, draped a tarp across that frame, and filled it with water to freeze. Hockey was not my strong suit. Think about it: if I couldn't walk on flat ground without falling over, there was no way I could stay standing on ice, even with the assistance of double-runner skates. With my temper and my drive to keep up with my brothers as my fuel, I usually laid sprawled out on the ice grasping for their ankles to trip them as they skated circles around me. I just wanted to be with my brothers and prove that I could compete with them. It was my way of staying in the game.

I loved my brothers. But I do not know if I could say that I loved them in the midst of the "torture" sessions. I would get so angry I would see red at times. But shortly after it was over, I forgave them, and we would start all over. Two of us were fine together—peaceful even—but add in the third and trouble would follow. They challenged me. They made me work. They "tortured" me, yes, but if any of the other kids on the block tried anything, they had my back. Only my brothers could give me a hard time.

I don't know if it was stubbornness and perfectionism or the desire to show my brothers I could do it, but as I grew older I could hold my own with them. I almost always lost, but I slowly started to get better. Little by little, I began to mature and become a better athlete—much to everyone's surprise.

* * *

We grew up in a happy household. Our first home was a very modest two-bedroom, one-bathroom home in Joliet, Illinois, which is about thirty miles southwest of Chicago. My brothers and I shared a bedroom with bunk beds and a trundle bed that would roll under the lower bunk. The neighborhood was full of children, so there was always a game going on somewhere. When the weather was nice, we never wanted to be inside, so we usually played from sunrise to sundown. Mom made us stop for lunch, which we weren't too happy about because we just wanted to keep playing. In the evening, we would hear Dad's whistle and immediately drop what we were doing and run home. We knew that if he whistled and we didn't come, we would be in trouble. Dad was the disciplinarian. Mom was the nurturer.

When I turned five years old, we were getting too big to share the same room, so my parents bought a three-bedroom house just over a mile from our first home in Joliet. This house had a full basement, which we quickly fell in love with because we could keep playing sports regardless of the weather. Hockey nets, a pinball machine that Brock had won in a contest, and other games were set up down there right away. We continued to be a family that revolved around sports. Usually, whatever sport was in season we were playing, inside or outside. Our yard was always the neighborhood playground for baseball, basketball, tetherball, football—whatever we could do. The games kept us together and they kept us safe. Our parents always knew where we were because all they had to do was look out through the window that we had just broken.

When I was about ten years old, my family built a new house in Joliet. It was on a street that only had nine houses at the time. The neighborhood, surrounded by cornfields, eventually expanded to twelve houses. It was a community where everyone was welcome into one another's homes, making it a very happy place to grow up. Enough kids lived in the neighborhood to play pick-up baseball and basketball games. A dirt lot next to our house became the infield for our baseball diamond, and the yards of neighboring houses became the left, center, and right fields. Our house served as the clubhouse where drinks and food were always available. Baselines were soon visible from so much use.

Every day of the summer we were out there. The kids would just show up, divide into teams, and play the rest of the day. On rainy days, we would beg Mom to let us go out and practice our sliding in the mud. We would come in muddy head to toe and soaked to the bone, but we loved it. Mom really did not mind. She was the perfect mom for boys. If we could not be on our diamond due to the weather, we would play the APBA baseball dice game or the Strat-O-Matic board game.

If only two of us were available to play baseball outside, I stood in front of the garage, bat in hand, as my brother or neighbor pitched the ball as hard as they could. We always found a way to play, no matter what the circumstances were. We all improved our skills in these pick-up games. When we were not playing baseball, it was basketball or hockey. When we broke a window, Dad put in a new one. He always kept extra windows and lightbulbs in the house for that reason.

Much to my advantage, my brothers' torture paid off. They had pushed me so hard that by the time I entered organized baseball at age seven, I was one of the best players. I was always advanced for my age group, and the awkward, tripping-over-himself kid was long gone. We played in city baseball leagues over the summer and on school teams in the fall; winter was saved for basketball. My elementary school had baseball teams starting in the fifth grade, which Dad would sometimes help coach. We were undefeated in my eighth-grade year and went on to win the state championship.

In the final game of the tournament, I threw a no-hitter, which only added to our championship celebration. It seemed to me that my baseball career was going to hinge around being a pitcher, but I eventually transitioned to being an infielder. When I realized that, in college and beyond, pitchers only played every four or five games, I preferred to play every day as an infielder and hitter. However, the no-hitter was near perfection in that eighth-grade game, and perfection is what I desired.

My mom loved raising boys, and she understood boys well. She realized that we needed to play, get dirty, and expend energy—and she loved it. She would be the first one out there playing with us and going to our games. At least one of our parents would go to all our games, no matter where we were playing. I am not sure how they did it with the three of us. Sometimes Dad was coaching two of our teams during the same season. I am grateful that our parents were so involved, supportive, and interested in everything that we did. They encouraged us to do our best. They allowed us to fail in sports and to learn valuable lessons through those failures. They allowed us to live and were not overprotective. They were neither helicopter parents (those who hover over their children) nor Zamboni parents (those who clear the path before their children so they never can fall).

My parents allowed us to learn difficult life lessons, which I have come to genuinely appreciate as an adult. They gave us, as the saying goes, "enough rope with which to hang yourself." They saw to it that we had a lot of freedom to make mistakes, but they wouldn't let us crash and burn. Mom and Dad also taught us responsibility and perseverance. If we signed up for something, we had to finish it. For example, when I was in the third grade, the high school was performing the play *The Music Man*, and they needed children that could sing in a few scenes. I tried out and got selected. About a week into it, I decided I did not like it and did not want to go to all the practices. Mom said, "You committed to this, so you are going to finish it." I did not like it at the time, but that lesson was really important. There are always things in life that you are not going to like, but you have to learn how to keep pushing forward.

Our parents saw to it that we had everything we needed to play hard and have fun, including their unceasing support. They knew the great lessons that we would learn from playing the games, negotiating our disagreements, using our imaginations, and working hard to achieve a dream. Other life lessons that they taught us included respecting our elders—like one unhappy neighbor we had woken up with a baseball flying through his bedroom window—and being kind to everyone. Although we were not a church-going family, we were taught strong, old-fashioned morals, especially how to treat others fairly and charitably.

I believe that my brothers and I grew up in an idyllic home. My brothers would tell you the same thing today. Sure, we fought a lot, and our family was by no means perfect, but our parents loved us and treated us generously. However, our story really started back in 1955 in Pinckneyville, a small farming community in southern Illinois, where our parents met.

* * *

Tod Masters' mother, Isabelle, was a schoolteacher and his father, Vernon, was a mechanic and coal miner. They encouraged their three sons to get a good education so that they wouldn't have to work manual labor their entire lives like their father had. Tod's mother was very involved in the United Church of Christ, playing the organ there for more than thirty years, and his father would occasionally attend. They raised their boys with strong discipline and encouraged them not only in their studies but also their athletic endeavors.

Tod excelled in basketball and baseball from a very young age. Pinckneyville High School, even though a very small school in a town of about three thousand people, was known far and wide for its basketball. Tod and all the young boys around town dreamed that they could play for the high school team. During his junior year at Pinckneyville High School, at the most important game of his high school athletic career, Tod met a young freshman named Janet Millikin. That night, Tod told his mother that he had met his future wife.

Janet was a beautiful young girl from Rice, a small farming community about nine miles north of Pinckneyville. Her parents, Frances and Charles, raised their five children with a strict upbringing in the Southern Baptist Church. Janet, the youngest child, was an athlete like Tod. Tod and Janet were both raised in strict Christian homes with strong moral teachings. Both families expected that their children would find a good Protestant to marry one day. Grandpa Charlie was happy that Janet found Tod. He loved that he was both a good basketball player and a Christian.

Tod and Janet dated through their high school years. They both knew that one day they would marry. Even though women were not encouraged to play sports as they are today, Janet played half-court basketball and enjoyed practicing with her older brother Tom, who was a basketball standout as well. Tod received a scholarship to play at Mississippi State University. He did not like being so far from Janet, but he wanted to pursue his dream of playing basketball at the college level.

Tod played for a great team at MSU, one that was ranked nationally. However, he did not like the way black people were treated in the South. And he began to miss Janet. After his second year of college, Tod had had enough and came home to Pinckneyville to stay. He began working at the family service station. Soon he became an excellent mechanic like his father. He earned the nickname "Doc" for his ability to fix cars. He had written letters to Janet during his time at MSU, so when he came back, they happily continued to date.

Tod and Janet were married on March 29, 1959, in the United Church of Christ. They began their married life in Pinckneyville and soon welcomed my oldest brother, Brock. Tod and Janet had always wanted to have a large family, and they were ecstatic when they became pregnant again in 1961. Janet always said that she only wanted boys. She loved sports and always felt comfortable doing all the things that boys did. She got her wish of only having boys, but it was not easy. Their second pregnancy ended with a stillborn baby boy that they named Michael. They never really talked about it much, but I know it was very hard on Mom.

My brother Blaine was born in 1964. He was a healthy baby boy that brought great joy back into the household. After my birth on December 17, 1966, Mom lost a lot of calcium. She had other physical complications, resulting in a hysterectomy. She would never be able to have more children, which was exceedingly difficult for her. One way or another, our family was complete. Four boys—three on earth and one with God in heaven.

Meanwhile, work was scarce in Pinckneyville, so Dad began looking for work outside the area in order to support his new family. He found it in Joliet, Illinois, eventually meeting up with a friend who wanted to go into business with him. They purchased their first Shell service station, where Dad worked as a mechanic. As business grew, they eventually bought another station in town. Life was busy for the new Masters family.

Both Dad and Mom had grown up in strong religious families. They had gone to church just about every Wednesday and Sunday. However, when they moved to Joliet, they fell out of practice. Maybe it was because they felt that their parents forced religion on them or because Dad's heavy work schedule often had him working seven days a week. Whatever the reason, they stopped going to church. They lost themselves in making a living and raising a family. But we always attended church when we visited my grandparents, which was once or twice a year.

I also remember going to Mass on special occasions with my Aunt Judi Masters, a cradle Catholic, who had married my dad's brother, Terry. They lived near us in Joliet and eventually moved across the street from us. Aunt Judi was the only Catholic in our family for many years. She raised their two boys, my cousins Mark and Michael, in the Catholic Church.

Throughout my childhood, religion was not a priority for our family, even though faith was especially important for my grandparents. I vaguely remember praying before Mom put us to bed. Above our beds hung a picture of a man steering a boat with Jesus behind him and guiding him. And we had on our coffee table a Bible that never was opened. I did not feel close to God at all in those early years. I did not understand what religion was all about, so I didn't pay much attention to it.

My brothers and I didn't grow up in a faith-filled environment. I see families today who teach their children to pray and who are at church weekly or even daily. They grow up with an intimate relationship with Jesus, which I never had. I do not begrudge my parents for it because it all worked out in the end for me. My lack of formation in the faith as a child could have pushed me to search for it later in life. But God is providential and cares for us every step of the way, even when we do not realize it. In my childhood, God was some distant entity that was important to my aunt and my grandmothers, but not to my immediate family. But at that point in my life, my only devotion was to playing sports.

* * *

My brothers and I attended Oak Valley and Laraway public schools in Joliet through the eighth grade, where we were all active in sports, especially baseball and basketball. I was a good student and I loved school, especially math. Having seen what caused my brothers to get in trouble at home and at school, I avoided those behaviors at all costs. I followed all the rules to a T. I was obedient to my parents and my teachers. I never wanted to mess up. I had to be perfect.

Sports and school allowed me to make some good friends, but I did not let anyone get too close to me. I did not like who I was on the inside, so I decided I was going to be perfect on the outside. I convinced myself that only then would everyone like me. I wanted to be the perfect student and the perfect athlete. In both areas I started to get attention, and this only fueled my desire for greater perfection. I thought that if I let anyone know the real me, they would surely run away and not want to be my friend. I certainly did not know who I was at this point in my life. My identity and my worth came from being a good student and a good baseball player.

Dad worked long hours so that Mom could stay at home and raise us. With all the struggle my parents went through raising the three of us, they never let it stop them from making us feel important. Mom was especially good at this. If you ever needed to talk to her, she made you feel like you were the only person that existed. I never felt like I had to compete for her attention because the instant she spoke to me or looked at me, I knew that I was important, valued, and, most of all, loved. She loved the three of us fiercely, and her example taught me how to love.

I was with Mom the day that I realized what my dream and destiny would be. I was about seven when she took my brothers and me to a Cubs game at Wrigley Field. Dad had to work. Because they grew up in southern Illinois, my parents were both diehard fans of the St. Louis Cardinals. They despised the Cubs—also known as the "loveable losers." We regularly watched them on Chicago's WGN TV station, and we rooted for whoever was playing against them. I cannot remember who the Cubs were playing that first time we went, but I still remember how enthralled I was by the sights, the sounds, the smells, and the game.

The freshly cut grass, the crack of the bat, the stacked hot dogs, the cheers of the crowd, the bright sunshine, and the pure athleticism of the players on the field drew me. I thought to myself, "This is what I want to do when I grow up." I wanted to be a part of this atmosphere forever. If I could play baseball and make a living doing it, that would be perfect. That day, like millions of young boys in America, I decided I was going to be a Major League Baseball player. I said to myself, "I'm going to be on this field one day."

So I dedicated myself to becoming the best player I could be. Baseball became my passion. I kept score at home while watching the Cubs games. I played whenever I could. I ate, slept, breathed, and lived baseball.

It was decided: I was destined for the majors.

CHAPTER TWO

MEETING JESUS

My parents sat down their thirteen-year-old son for what appeared to be an important conversation. What they told me was a complete surprise.

"Catholic school?" I asked again. "You want *me*"—I pointed at myself for emphasis—"to go to a Catholic school?" This was something they had been thinking about for a while, but I had been completely unaware. I couldn't believe it.

"It's either Joliet Catholic or Providence, Burke," Dad said.

My parents explained that they weren't happy with the public high school's baseball program. Both Catholic schools in the area were known both for academic and athletic excellence, as well as discipline and family atmosphere. Even as an eighth grader, I knew that this would be a significant financial expense for my parents. We didn't have a lot of money, but my parents were willing to make this sacrifice for me and my future. I was touched that my parents even considered it. They believed in me. Dad said that he knew I had a shot at playing college baseball and maybe even further. And either one of these schools would help me get there. Now all that was left was to choose between Joliet Catholic and Providence.

Even though recruiting was not allowed, I heard from the baseball coaches at both Catholic high schools. I was honored that both coaches took a special interest in inviting me to different events. Providence invited me to a basketball game where I sat with the dean and some of my baseball friends. We watched a great Providence team—led by Walter Downing, who would go on to play at Marquette and DePaul—dominate the court. The crowd was electric and the feeling in the gym made me feel like I was at home. Although I had enjoyed my visit to Joliet Catholic, that night I decided to spend the next four years at Providence and began to prepare myself for success.

* * *

The dean explained to me that, even though I wasn't Catholic, I would have to attend the all-school Masses and take the theology courses. I didn't mind. I was willing to do whatever it took to further my baseball career and to get a good education. I had nothing against Catholicism. I just didn't know much about it. That didn't make seeing multiple priests and religious sisters on staff any less intimidating. I had never been that close to a priest or religious sister before, other than seeing them while attending an occasional Mass with my Aunt Judi. But at Providence they were walking the halls and teaching classes.

When I entered the school that first day as a freshman, I was scared to death. My fear didn't last long, as the atmosphere of Providence made me feel like I belonged. Although I had enjoyed my public school experience, this was different. Providence seemed to radiate a family-like spirit. Even though I knew my teachers had cared about me in grade school, the teachers at Providence took it to a higher level. The students cared for one another, and the teachers cared for us like we were their own children. I was drawn into that environment and loved it.

My confidence plummeted, however, when I walked into my freshman theology class. As a child, I had heard some stories about Jesus, so I thought I knew a little about the Bible. I was a good student, and I believed I could figure it out. I soon realized I was way behind the curve. My classmates, many of whom had gone to Catholic grade school, seemed to know everything about the faith and the Bible. On top of it all, a religious sister taught the class. Her name was Sr. Margaret Anne. She wasn't mean or scary—in fact, she was incredibly kind—but I was intimidated by her spirituality. When she looked at you, she seemed to look right into your soul. So, naturally, I tried to blend into the wall. I listened intently but feared that at any moment she would ask me a simple question that I wouldn't be able to answer. My biggest worry was being embarrassed in front of my peers for not knowing a basic tenet of the faith.

Sister must have sensed my anxiety because she never put me on the spot. I was always striving for perfection in the classroom, always at the top of my class, but I was way out of my league here. At the same time, the theology class intrigued me, and I found myself drawn to Jesus and the teachings of the Catholic Church.

Sr. Margaret Anne would stand at the doorway at the end of class and say goodbye to each of us. One day, I was the last one left after the bell rang, and I knew something was going to happen when I saw Sister waiting for me. "How can I sneak by her without any interaction?" I thought, dreading walking through the door.

I was a very shy teenager. I didn't like the person that I was. I often walked the halls with my head down so that no one would look me in the eye. I feared that they would see the real me and run away. I put my books under my arm, bowed my head, and began walking toward the door, hoping that she wouldn't notice me. As I tried to pass by her, Sister stopped me. She raised my chin, looked me in the eye, and said, "Burke, you are searching for something." I didn't know how to react, so I smiled, put my head back down, and tried to walk away. She stopped me again and gave me a Bible. "Start reading the Gospel of Matthew," she said.

"Thank you," I said, accepting her gift and walking quickly away.

What just happened? Her suspicion about me made sense. I guess I'd always known I was searching for something but had never been able to put into words what I was feeling. I was searching—but for what? And better yet, how did she know? And where in the Bible was the Gospel of Matthew? I was touched by her concern and thought she may be giving me answers to my deepest questions.

My mind raced during baseball practice that afternoon. I went home, ate dinner, did my homework, and went to my room. I shut the door because I didn't want my brothers to know what I was doing. They knew that I was a good student and that I would study anything my teachers told me to. But I didn't want to have to explain that I couldn't wait to get to the Bible. I found the Gospel of Matthew and began to read the Bible for the first time in my life.

Even though I had what seemed like an idyllic upbringing, nobody's life is perfect and nobody is without sin. I knew I was a sinner, and I honestly believed I was the only one. Was I the only one with a messed-up life? I thought that if people knew who I was—*really* knew—they'd run. I was still growing into my identity. Who was I? Was I the result of all my past mistakes? Was I the combination of all my sins? That's why I unconsciously became a perfectionist. I thought that if I became this person that everyone liked, if I portrayed this perfect image, if I became this person that others wanted me to be, everyone, including God, would love me. Looking back, I realize how much I wanted to be known and to be loved. I couldn't have articulated that at the time, but I was searching.

I didn't read much that first night, but I enjoyed what I read. I decided I would read a little bit more every night until I got through the Gospel. My heart was open, and I started to hope that Jesus was going to give me what I had been searching for. As the weeks passed, I felt lighter each time I read the Scriptures. I looked forward to the time I got to spend with the Bible. When I read about Jesus dying on the cross, I sensed great peace and joy. I realized that if Jesus willingly died on the cross to save me, it demanded a response from me. At the time, I didn't know what Jesus would ask of me. But I felt a peace and joy that I had never experienced before. The seeds of my vocation were planted during that time of reading the Gospel of Matthew. Sr. Margaret Anne was right: I was searching for *something*. But not only that; I was searching for *someone*. I had found him, and I couldn't get enough. St. Augustine, in one of his most famous quotes, said, "We were made for you, Lord, and our hearts are restless until they rest in you." Looking back on my experience reading Scripture, I know that was happening in my heart. It had been restless for the first fifteen years of my life because it had never encountered Jesus. I'd tried to fill my heart with baseball, good grades, friends, and other things. None of those were bad things. It's just that my heart was longing for God, and now I had found him. I knew that I liked what I was experiencing, and I wanted more. I continued to devour the material from the theology class and Scripture. I found that the heavy cloud that used to hang over me was lifting. Reading the Bible was consoling me, and I could not get enough.

Once a month, we celebrated an all-school Mass in the gym at Providence. I didn't know any of the Mass responses or when to sit or stand. I was very self-conscious that everyone was watching my every move, which of course was not true. Teenagers are generally self-conscious, but as a non-Catholic teenager in a Catholic school, the stress was even greater. I was not the only non-Catholic student, but when it came time for Communion, I felt like I was. I was sure that there was a spotlight on me with a bright flashing sign that read "sinner." When I remained in my seat and watched everyone else go receive the Host, I remember feeling embarrassed and out of place.

After a few months, I stopped focusing on myself and started to pay attention to what was happening at Mass. I couldn't understand why my friends received Communion so reverently. It looked like ordinary bread and wine. Although I didn't understand it, I wanted to participate in Communion. Sr. Margaret Anne taught that the Eucharist truly was the Body and Blood of Jesus, but I couldn't wrap my head around it. On one hand, I thought the Catholics were crazy believing that the Host was the real Body and Blood of Jesus. On the other hand, my heart was being drawn into the mystery. All I knew was that I wanted to learn about it and experience it.

* * *

I continued to excel in academics and in baseball. By my sophomore year I was among the top of my class academically. I was on the varsity baseball team, starting at second base and batting second in the lineup. That sophomore year I batted .450, broke state records, and received attention locally and nationally. My brothers took it upon themselves to keep me humble. If they saw my name in a newspaper, they would make sure to do or say something to keep me grounded. They wanted to make sure that "my head would fit through the door."

Even though I was still rather shy, my friendships grew and deepened. One of our teachers, Joe Rodeghero, and his wife, Debbie, invited some of my friends to their house for dinner and a card game. Today, this would be unheard of, but in the 1980s it was commonplace. Joe was a teacher and coach at Providence. I never had the chance to play on one of Joe's teams because we were always at different levels, but he was one of my favorite teachers.

My friends and I joined Joe and Deb at their home, which students called "The Bat Cave" because it was tucked back at the end of a dead-end street. We had a great time, enjoyed a nice dinner, and played some games afterward. I was impressed because

the Rodegheros were normal and yet took their faith seriously.
Sometimes I would visit them with my classmates. Sometimes
I would visit them alone. I began going to Mass with them on
Sundays and accompanying them to some family gatherings. I had
a preconceived idea that religious people were weird or boring.
But they enjoyed life and sports and at the same time tried to live
moral lives and do things the right way.

Over time, I developed a close relationship with them and
became an honorary member of their family. I loved being with
my family, but I also loved being around a family that practiced
their faith. Joe and I began to call each other friends, and I started
visiting them without my classmates. Their daughter, Christa,
was about three years old when I began to visit their home. It
was great to watch her grow up, as I never had younger siblings.

* * *

A decision during my junior year at Providence changed my life
forever. I went on a Kairos retreat with about twenty of my male
classmates. One of the mottos of the retreat was "God doesn't
make junk." Until then, I hadn't realized that that was what
I had always believed: that I was junk, no good, and that God
could never love someone like me. The retreat was amazing. At
one of the Masses, the priest invited us around the altar for the
consecration and Communion. I had never met the priest and
I had never been that close to the altar before. To be so near to
the "action" of the Mass had a deep impact on me. I had never
felt so close to God.

When it came time for Communion, instead of us forming a
line to go to the priest, he came around the semicircle to each one
of us. He started on the other side, so I had time to think about
what was going to happen. I had never been in a Communion
line before. I wasn't aware that I could cross my hands in front
of my chest to ask for a blessing. When the priest came to me,

he raised the Host and said, "The Body of Christ," and I froze. I opened my mouth to say, "I am not Catholic," but the words did not come out, and the priest placed the Host on my tongue. He didn't know that he had just given me my First Communion. I was not even baptized.

Immediately, I sensed power go through my body. My head was spinning. What just happened? I felt the power of God go through my body in a way that I had never experienced before. I knew in my heart that I had just received the Body of Christ. It was a surreal experience. I floated through the rest of the Mass and the retreat. There were so many wonderful experiences at the retreat, from the talks by the adults and my peers to the prayer and the Masses. But the intimate moment with Jesus in the Eucharist was the highlight. I went home after the retreat and excitedly shared the details with my parents.

"I think I have to join the Catholic Church," I said, after I had recounted the Communion experience. Wisely, my parents did not let me jump too quickly, as I was only seventeen years old.

My mother looked at me kindly. "You need to pray and study," she said. "When you're eighteen, if this is what you want to do, we'll support you."

I think my parents regretted not raising us in any faith. They always told us that when we were eighteen, we could choose the faith that we wanted to practice. Many parents do not want to force religion on their children. I find it interesting that we indoctrinate our children into becoming fans of our favorite sports teams, but we do not want to lead them into our faith. I would not recommend this hands-off approach to parents regarding religion. But somehow, by the grace of God, this method worked out in my family.

My parents told me to take the next year to pursue learning more about the Catholic faith and praying about whether I was being called to join. After a year of praying and studying, if I still wanted to become Catholic, they would support me one hundred percent.

I contacted Fr. Mike at Providence. He was an Augustinian priest that everyone loved. I found it easy to talk to him about matters of faith. I met with him one-on-one weekly and asked him questions that I couldn't bring myself to ask in theology class in front of my peers. Fr. Mike, like my mother, kept encouraging me to study and pray. And the more I studied and prayed, the more I wanted to become Catholic. It all made sense. Not only was the faith logical, which I appreciated because I liked math and science, but the Church was so welcoming to me. I was also drawn by the fact that the Catholic Church could trace its history back to the time of Christ. There were also so many brilliant people and saints who chose to be Catholic and who wrote eloquently about the faith. I desired to be a part of it all.

* * *

Near the end of my junior year in high school, I received letters from college baseball coaches. Today, this process of recruiting can begin in elementary school for some players, but in the 1980s, they began recruiting in the later years of high school. Schools I had never heard of contacted me, wanting me to play baseball for them. My parents talked to several professional scouts. I was amazed by all the attention, but I tried not to let it affect me too much. I tried to be the best player I could be while maintaining a humble attitude. After talking with many coaches and doing some research, I narrowed down my options to three schools: Northwestern, Mississippi State, and Stanford. I wanted a good school with an excellent baseball program where I could study math, my favorite subject.

Northwestern would have been perfect because it was close to home and had an incredible reputation for academics. Joe Girardi was the catcher for Northwestern and was assigned to be my host for the weekend. The visit was spoiled by snow. I was tired of the cold weather and practicing inside for so many years. I decided that weekend that Northwestern was not in my future.

The next trip my parents and I made was to Mississippi State, where Dad played college basketball. The weather was completely different. It was sunny and eighty degrees at the March game, with ten thousand people in attendance. College baseball was a lifestyle in Starkville. I could sense it in the air. A great energy filled the crowd watching the game that day, and it felt like home. Playing for MSU that day were Will Clark, Rafael Palmeiro, Bobby Thigpen, and Jeff Brantley—all future big leaguers. Playing for Auburn, their opponent, was Bo Jackson, a future professional baseball and football player. I could see my dream materializing before my eyes. Coach Polk made a nice offer, and I made my decision. I canceled the trip to Stanford. I was going to play as a Mississippi State Bulldog! Now that the pressure of choosing a college was out of the way, I could concentrate on having a great senior season of baseball at Providence.

I received many local and state honors for baseball. One personal honor came after my junior year. I was selected to be on Team Chicago, an all-star team that toured the Netherlands and Germany for two weeks during the summer. We played baseball with local club teams and shared goodwill with everyone that we met. It was an amazing experience. With three successful seasons of high school baseball under my belt, I was very excited about my senior season. I didn't have to worry about impressing college coaches. I could relax and play.

I was itching to get back on the field, but I was even more excited for what this year would mean. After my intense year of discernment, I knew that I was called to be Catholic. I felt at home when I entered a Catholic church, especially sensing the power of the Blessed Sacrament. Before I made it official, the school asked me during my senior year to lead one of the Kairos retreats. They told me that I was the first non-Catholic to be the main leader for a Kairos at Providence. I was honored. I remember the joy of witnessing the power of the Holy Spirit working in the lives of many of my classmates. It was my first taste of ministry, and I loved it. At this time, I never imagined myself being a priest because I was so focused on baseball. But the retreat planted a seed deep in my soul. I was amazed that God used me to help others come to know him personally. I understood the saying, "It is better to give than to receive," especially as it applies to matters of faith. I knew more than ever that I was meant to become Catholic, and I asked Fr. Mike to baptize me.

* * *

I learned that it was the custom to have at least one godparent. I knew who I wanted to choose. Joe Rodeghero and I had developed a deep friendship. We had built a trusting relationship to the point that one evening I opened up to him about everything that I had kept hidden and thought that I would take to my grave without ever sharing with anyone. For the first time, someone saw me for who I really was. I was far from the perfect image that I had tried to portray. Joe didn't even blink an eye. He saw *me* and still loved me. He didn't run like I thought he would. It was my first glimpse of God the Father's unconditional love. Joe helped dispel the lie that if someone really knew me, especially the ugly parts of my life, they would judge me harshly and flee. His unconditional love and acceptance were an example that I have tried to follow throughout my life. To this day, I try to build relationships of trust and share vulnerably with friends. This was a life-changing lesson. It has also helped me love and accept others now when they share with me their struggles and sins.

I would have loved to have Joe's wife Deb be my godmother, but the day I was baptized she was in the hospital to give birth to their son, Zachary. In an honorary way, she has always been my godmother. The Baptism took place in the chapel at Providence, and Fr. Mike was the presider. My parents and brothers were there along with my aunt and uncle and a few friends from school. It was an intimate setting for a life-changing event. Fr. Mike traced the sign of the cross on my forehead, and Joe followed suit. I had come to embrace Jesus as my Savior, who died on the cross for my sins. Until May 26, 1985—five years to the day before my grand slam against Florida State—I was a creation of God. But on this special day, as Fr. Mike poured the water over my head, the Holy Spirit descended upon me, and I believe God claimed me as his beloved son, even though it would take a while for me to fully embrace this identity. Father placed a white garment over my head, showing me that I had been washed clean from original sin and all my personal sins. I never realized how much sin had weighed me down until I felt the freedom of the baptismal grace wash over me.

Joe received the baptismal candle that was lit from the Easter candle. Father told us to keep this flame of faith alive in our hearts. I still have that candle as a reminder of what Christ did for me that day. Although I didn't grasp the full meaning at the time, this day set the course for the rest of my life. Every year, I now try to celebrate May 26: the day my Baptism changed my identity forever. It is more important to me than December 17, the day of my birth.

With my Baptism, high school had come to an end. I signed a national letter of intent to play baseball at Mississippi State University. College baseball was waiting for me.

CHAPTER THREE

A CHANGE OF PLANS

Mississippi State University is in the town of Starkville, which was a culture shock to me, coming from Joliet. I had to attune my ears to a different accent. I was delighted by the friendliness and hospitality of the people. And I discovered that God has a sense of humor. I grew up as a non-Catholic in Joliet, which was probably fifty to sixty percent Catholic. Then, as a three-month-old baptized Catholic, I found myself in Mississippi, where it was two percent Catholic. The Bible Belt hit me full force. I was a religious minority once again.

My parents drove me to Starkville and helped me move into McArthur Hall, which was the athletic dorm on campus. Freshman orientation went by in a blur. On the first day, I met Jody Hurst, a teammate who would become my best friend in college. Jody was a kind, laid back, tall and lanky center fielder from Meridian, Mississippi. Even though we had just met, I knew I had met a friend for life and felt comfortable with him right away. Everything I was experiencing at MSU was new and exciting. This was the next step in the plan to achieve my lifelong dream of playing in the Major Leagues.

Although my main goal was baseball, my parents had instilled in their sons the importance of getting an education. My father did not want us doing manual labor our whole lives like he did.

Choosing a major got me thinking about life after my time as a professional baseball player. Maybe I'd be a teacher or a doctor. I had always loved animals and considered being a veterinarian. I wasn't sure, so I started off in something that I liked and that had always come easy: math.

In the dorm, the football players lived on the second, third, and fourth floors. Basketball and tennis players took the fifth floor, and our baseball team and some golfers lived on the sixth floor. Academics wasn't the priority for many of the men in the athletic dorm, but it was important to me. I wanted a quality education. My parents knew that I pushed myself hard academically, and they encouraged me to relax. They stressed that getting a B in a class was not the end of the world. By his loving me despite my flaws, my godfather Joe taught me that I didn't have to be perfect, but this perfectionistic trait was entrenched in me. The desire to be a perfect athlete and a perfect student compelled me. I got my identity from my performance on the field and in the classroom, and it was growing stronger.

A few other guys in my dorm made academics a priority, and we banded together. When a lot of the other guys would go out partying, we would stay in the dorm to study and socialize. I was never into the party scene, even in high school. I found that you don't need alcohol to have a good time.

Although I had just completed a great four-year Catholic education, I didn't know how to defend my faith, and it got challenged a lot in Mississippi. One of our coaches, Brian Shoop, was a strong Christian and led a Bible study for the players on Saturday mornings at seven o'clock. I went because I wanted to learn more about Jesus and Scripture. My teammates often asked me questions about the Catholic faith like: "How can you believe that the Eucharist is really the Body and Blood of Christ? Why do you confess your sins to a priest instead of going directly to God?" I'd think, "I don't know why we believe that; we just do." I was grateful for the questioning because it made me investigate why we believe what we believe. If I had gone to a Catholic university, I probably would not have been challenged to grow in my faith the way I was at MSU.

At one of the Bible studies, one of my teammates asked me why Catholics worship Mary and the saints. He quoted 1 Timothy 2:5: "There is also one mediator between God and humankind, Christ Jesus."

"Let me go and study," I said, "and I will let you know next week." I knew some Catholic teaching, but I wasn't well formed. I did not have all the answers at my fingertips. So I went back to Scripture and my *Catechism*, and I consulted a priest from back home.

At the Bible study the next week, I explained that we don't worship Mary or the saints. "We honor Mary as the mother of Jesus," I said. "Jesus was a good Jewish man who followed all the commandments, including the fourth commandment to honor your father and mother. Catholics honor Mary in a similar way. We believe that she is in heaven with Jesus and the saints, and we ask them to intercede for us."

"If I were sick," I said, "I would ask you to pray for me. Can I go right to Jesus with my prayer intentions? Of course, and I do. But I can ask for your prayers too. Do you believe that your prayers have meaning with God?"

"Yes," my teammate replied, "I believe in the power of prayer."

"The Catholic Church teaches that Mary and the saints are with God in heaven," I said. "And we can ask them to pray for us just like I would ask you to pray for me. It certainly can't hurt to have many people praying for the same intention, especially when they are so close to God!"

I had many conversations like this with my friends and teammates over the years at MSU. While they may not have always agreed with what I shared about what the Catholic Church teaches, they could at least understand the logic behind it. All their questions helped strengthen my own faith and formation. For that I will always be grateful.

At the same time, I was questioning myself: Why were there so few Catholics in Mississippi? I enjoyed being around these good people. Maybe I was missing something? Maybe Fr. Mike and Sr. Margaret Anne left something out when they taught me? After all, the Catholic Church was the only place that I received any formal religious education.

I admired one of the graduate assistant coaches, Mike Hutcheon or "Hutch," a strong Christian man who took his faith very seriously. He challenged me to grow in faith, introduced me to contemporary Christian music, and invited me to go to the Baptist church with him. He encouraged me to bring my Bible and a pen to take notes, which I did. I enjoyed their services very much. The music was beautiful and the preaching was inspirational. But I went back to St. Joseph Catholic Church to receive the Eucharist. I attended other Protestant churches with Jody and friends, trying to find my spiritual home. Baptist, Methodist, Lutheran, Pentecostal—you name it, I tried it. And every time I found the service meaningful and the people great, but something very important was always missing: Holy Communion.

I learned that the Catholic Church is the only church that believes in the abiding, Real Presence of Jesus in the Eucharist. Each time after attending the other churches, I raced to Mass to receive the Eucharist. Many college kids stop going to church once they move out of their homes and into a dorm, but I was going to church twice on Sundays. After three semesters of searching, I stopped going to the other churches and only attended St. Joseph's. None of the other churches could fulfill me the way the Eucharist did at Mass.

I didn't have a full understanding of God, the Mass, and the Eucharist. I knew that there was something very special in the Eucharist, but I didn't grasp its depth and its beauty. I went to

Sunday Mass because I knew it was the right thing to do, and I felt better after going. I did not go out of obligation; I wanted to be there. I felt close to God, but I had not yet learned how to pray or to have a personal relationship with him. I didn't know about the abundant graces that God wants to give us in the Eucharist. It wasn't until I went to the seminary about ten years later that I began to appreciate everything about the Catholic Church. I now see each sacrament as a personal encounter with Jesus. If I knew then what I know now, I would have gone to Mass every day. I only knew that I was called to be Catholic and always would be.

* * *

At the first workouts when I got to campus, I realized how important baseball was at MSU. I knew it was a big deal, but it surprised me to see about a hundred guys walk on the field that first day to try to make the team. I had a scholarship, so I was confident that I would make it. But after I watched the tryouts, I was intimidated. At the first open tryout, I went out to second base and a bunch of guys joined me. Every one of them was very talented. Five of us had been named all-state in high school in our respective states. Day by day, Coach Polk and his staff whittled the team down to forty men. There were about thirty scholarship players and the other ten were walk-ons. I was relieved to officially make the team. Then the real work began to make the starting lineup.

Through the fall, we played a lot of inner-squad scrimmages. Not only was I holding my own, but I was doing quite well. Coach Polk had an evaluation process in which the coaches ranked the position players from one to twenty-five and the pitchers from one to fifteen. The players would do the same thing. That fall of my freshman year, I was voted the fourth-best overall position player on the team by my peers and number eight by the coaching staff. I assumed this meant I would be starting, since I was the top-ranked second baseman on the team.

In November, Coach Polk called me into his office. "Burke, we're going to redshirt you," he said. I knew it was common to redshirt freshmen, which meant you could practice but not play in games. You were given five years to play four. Redshirting meant that you would have an extra year to mature. But I never thought that would pertain to me. I expected that since I had such a good fall, I would be in the starting lineup in the spring. Not every freshman was redshirted, and I believed I had earned the right to play.

"We've got a senior second baseman," he said, "so we're going to start him. Then, next year, you'll be a little older, a little more mature, and you'll have the next four years to play. This may hurt now, but you will appreciate it in the future."

We talked about it for a long time, but whatever reason he gave me, I didn't like it. I couldn't move past it. I thought about all the other places I could have gone and started as a freshman. The thought was festering when I flew home for Thanksgiving. In my mind, I had already transferred to the University of St. Francis in Joliet, where I could be a starter that spring season. I must admit I was also homesick. Although I had made some good friends, I missed my family, Joe Rodeghero and his family, and my friends from home. All those feelings, combined with the news of being redshirted, had sealed the deal.

On the way home from the airport, I told Mom and Dad about my plans to transfer.

"I'm not going back," I said.

Dad laughed and said, "Oh yes you are! It will be the biggest mistake of your life if you quit now."

My parents had taught us to finish what we started; they did not raise quitters. They could see that I was about to make a big mistake if I reacted out of anger. By the end of the break, they had convinced me to return to Mississippi State. It didn't make that first spring season any easier to bear.

If it were not for my friends Jody and Russ Mahan, another Yankee from New Jersey, I would have had a hard time making it through that spring. Since the three of us were redshirted, Jody often invited us to his home in Meridian, Mississippi, on weekends to enjoy some home cooking from his wonderful mother. We'd listen to the games on the radio and wallow in our sorrows. We sat around Jody's girlfriend's swimming pool and talked about how we should have been playing. The MSU team did fairly well that 1986 season, finishing 34–21, but failed to make the playoffs.

I enjoyed bonding with these new friends. They helped me get over my homesickness that second semester of my freshman year. Much to my surprise, I started to feel at home in Starkville. That summer after freshman year, Jody and Russ came back to Joliet with me, and we had fun playing in a summer baseball league for men of all ages. It made us all the more excited for the next spring when our redshirts would be lifted and we could finally play in official games.

During my second year of college, what we called the redshirt-freshman year, I started at second base. Our third baseman, Pete Young, a true freshman, was our closing pitcher. Coach told me that whenever Pete came in to pitch, they were going to move me over to third and bring in another second basemen. I had never played third base, but I thought, "How hard could it be? It's just another infield position." The first time I was moved to third during the season, we were playing Auburn University, and we were up 5–2 in the 9th inning. The place was packed with at least ten thousand people, which was nearly half the population of Starkville.

As I took my position at third base, I saw Frank Thomas—soon to become the "Big Hurt" of the Chicago White Sox—who was 6′5″ and 240 pounds, in the batter's box. In his hands was an aluminum bat that looked like a toothpick. Coach had always told us to expect the ball so you were never surprised when it came your way. I was praying that Thomas wouldn't hit it to me.

Of course, he hit a hard ground ball to me that bounced off my chest, and I made an error. Now there was a man on first. The next guy hit a ball to my left—I was thinking double play—but I dropped the ball, and then there were men on first and second. The next ball was hit to my right—I was thinking triple play—but I dropped the ball. Eventually, all three guys came around to score. When we finally got out of the inning, the score was tied 5-5. Normally you don't hear individual voices with such a large crowd. You hear a general buzz. However, as I was running off the field, I distinctly heard one voice from this boisterous crowd yell, "We had to go all the way to Illinois to get this guy?" We ended up losing the game in fifteen innings a few hours later. I had failed my team and myself.

Current technology was not available in 1987, so my parents were not able to listen to or watch my games from Illinois. They anxiously awaited my calls after each game. "I quit, I'm terrible, and the people here hate me," I told my parents that night. I was devastated. I wanted so badly to succeed, and I had made a fool out of myself on the field. Baseball was no joke to the people of Starkville. It was no joke to me. I got my identity from how I played on the field, and I had played terribly. I was a failure. There was no way that I could redeem myself after such a horrible game—and in front of so many people! I was ready to quit again and come home to the local university. Once again, my parents talked me off the ledge.

"You had a bad game," Dad said. "Dust yourself off; tomorrow's a new day. That's the beauty of baseball. You don't have to wait too long to get back out there to redeem yourself."

Sometimes we need to be reminded that our mistakes are not insurmountable. We need to recognize that at times we make errors, but there's a chance for redemption. We sin and think that we're no good. We think that not even God can forgive us. But the Lord can't wait to forgive us and encourages us to start over. He tells us to dust ourselves off and get back in the game of life. Dad was teaching me an important life lesson and a deep spiritual lesson. Just as important, we need to be reminded that we shouldn't get our identity from what we do. When we get our identity from what we do, it is like riding an emotional roller coaster. I didn't learn this until much later, but when we accept our true identity as beloved children of God, life is still like a wild roller coaster, but we can experience a deep sense of peace during the ride.

After that debacle of a game against Auburn, I worked hard and tried not to let my performance on the field define who I was—without much success. I regularly went to Mass at St. Joseph parish in Starkville. Fr. Mike, a priest from Ireland, was the pastor, and he was a big baseball fan. He prayed for the team at Mass, and he asked me and Tommy Raffo, the other Catholic on the team, to stand up so people could applaud and wish us luck. Starkville was really a town built around a college campus, and they treated the student athletes like professionals. There was such incredible support behind the baseball team that I didn't want to let them down on or off the field. In Starkville, it was difficult to separate my identity from being a baseball player.

The 1987 Bulldogs team had an up-and-down year, which was to be expected because it was a freshmen-dominated team. We were young and inexperienced, but there was a lot of talent on the field. We struggled in SEC play, finishing sixth in the conference with a 13–13 record. Only six teams made the conference tournament, so we barely made it. However, we won the conference tournament in Athens, Georgia, beating teams like Louisiana State, which featured future major leaguer Albert Joey Belle, and Georgia, with future Major League pitchers Derek Lilliquist and Chris Carpenter. My friend Jody Hurst hit home runs off both of those pitchers in one game to help us win the tournament.

We were able to host an NCAA regional tournament in 1987. We were young and talented, and Starkville always attracted record crowds. A talented Oklahoma State team, featuring Robin Ventura, came to Starkville and won the regional tournament to go to the College World Series. Our MSU team finished with a respectable 39–22 record.

The 1988 season was even more exciting. We were all a year older with that year of experience under our belts. Inspired by our miraculous victory in the 1987 SEC tournament, we had more confidence entering the season. We finished third in the SEC in 1987 with a 17-10 record. We again hosted an NCAA regional tournament, which featured future MLB catcher Brent Mayne and the Cal State Fullerton Titans. Cal State won the regionals and did very well in the College World Series, but Stanford won the national championship that year. We finished with a respectable 44–20 record.

I played in the renowned Cape Cod summer collegiate league the summer of 1988. My teammates included Mo Vaughn and Chuck Knoblauch, both of whom starred in the MLB. We played against future stars like Frank Thomas and Jeff Bagwell. I was competing with the best players in the country and felt like I could play at their level.

* * *

My Catholicism was solidified in the Bible Belt. I continued to go to the Bible study on Saturdays and attend weekly Fellowship of Christian Athletes (FCA) meetings. I loved learning about Jesus and sharing with other believers. I also wanted to present a good image of the Catholic Church because there was so much misunderstanding about Catholics. Granted, some Catholics did not give the best witness of the faith. But I really wanted people to understand that Catholics are Christians as well, contrary to what some people believed.

One evening, I called home to talk to Mom about changing majors from mathematics to computer science, or double majoring in both. Both my brothers were at the house for dinner, so Mom relayed the message to them while we were talking.

As I related to her that I was thinking about changing majors, both brothers said in unison, "He's going to become a priest."

"No! I'm not going to become a priest," I said. "I'm just thinking about changing majors!"

Looking back on that conversation, I realize that other people saw something in me long before I saw it. Priesthood was not on my radar screen at all. I was going to play in the Major Leagues. After baseball, I was thinking about going into medicine, or teaching, or something to do with math. I pictured being a priest as a very boring life compared to a career in baseball. Many things had improved for me in baseball after that dreadful three-error performance at third base, and I wasn't about to give up on it.

In my junior year, I was named the CoSIDA Academic All-American Player of the Year, which is one of the biggest honors I received in college. Each conference names their player of the year, and I was the one selected for the whole country. It was both an academic and athletic honor, which reflected all the hard work I put into both disciplines. To carry a 4.0 GPA while playing major college baseball was a goal of mine, as I was striving for perfection. I studied on bus trips, and although math came easily to me, there was a lot of work involved. I still had the flawed belief that I had to be perfect for people to like me, to appreciate me, to love me. I didn't see the lie that I had embraced as a young child.

Although baseball and academics consumed much of my time, I did have a social life. I spent a lot of time with my friends on the team, especially Jody and Russ. Jody and I became roommates our second year, and we remained roommates through our third year. Our fourth year, Jody, Russ, and I teamed up with Bo McKinnis, another great friend, to rent an apartment. We lived, ate, and drank baseball. Bo was the equipment manager and introduced me to rotisserie baseball, now called fantasy baseball, which I still play to this day.

Around my senior year, I dated Connie, a good Methodist girl, who was also a math major. Connie loved baseball and math, and she was a beautiful Christian woman, so we got along well. We dated for a while, but it wasn't serious because I was focused on baseball. She would tell you the same thing. After we graduated, she moved to Atlanta, and we parted ways.

In 1989, the MSU baseball team was considered one of the best teams in the country. We were a group that had started together as freshmen in 1987, and this was our third year playing together. There was talent all around the diamond on that team. We were ranked at or near the top of all the national polls most of the season. We set the record for MSU with fifty-four wins that year. We won the SEC regular season with a record of 20–5. We entered the regionals with great confidence but sadly were upset by a tough North Carolina team that featured John Thoden, my teammate on the Wareham Gatemen the summer before in the Cape Cod League. We were all devastated because we thought the 1989 MSU team had a chance to win the national championship.

Many of our teammates were drafted by Major League teams after that season, so we were not highly touted in 1990. Nevertheless, we entered 1990, my senior season, with high hopes. Few people outside our locker room thought we had a chance because of all the great talent we lost the year before. But we all knew each other very well, and we played at a level beyond our talent because of the chemistry of the team. We won fifty games—one of only six MSU teams in the school's history to reach that milestone, including the 2021 National Championship MSU baseball team. We finished in third place in the SEC with a 17–9 record. We tied for first in the SEC tournament with LSU. Rain caused the championship game to be canceled, with the regional tournaments to begin soon afterward.

We were ready to host for the fourth year in a row the NCAA regional tournament. We defeated the University of Illinois and Brigham Young University to lead us into that memorable matchup with Florida State University. This was the game in which I hit my game-winning grand slam that has been voted the number one sports moment in Mississippi State history.

I remember walking off the field that day, after going 6 for 6 and hitting a grand slam, whispering to my good friend and coach Russ McNickle, "I can't believe I just did that."

He laughed, "Me either."

As I drove home that night down the main commercial street in Starkville, several of the restaurant marquees read, "Way to go Burke!" I could not believe what was happening. Was I dreaming, or did that really happen? Even now, when I go back to Mississippi, people tell me where they were when I hit the grand slam. People say that they almost drove off the road listening to it on the radio. Almost everyone says they were at the game. If everyone who said they were there had been there, it would be close to fifty thousand people. I've even had a few different people say that they got the ball!

We had to win another game to make it to the College World Series. Florida State won their next game against Illinois and then had to beat us twice to get to Omaha. They beat us the next game 11–8, and so it came down to a deciding one-game playoff. We won the final 4–3 in an exciting back and forth game, and we were off to Omaha! I was voted most valuable player of the tournament after going 12 for 14 in the first three games, and 14 for 22 in the series. I could not wait to play in the College World Series, which was one of my goals as a young boy when I imagined playing college baseball.

I think this regional tournament was God's way of saying, "Enjoy this, Burke. This is your moment. Soak it in." I didn't realize until years later that the grand slam occurred on the fifth anniversary of my Baptism. I don't think it was a coincidence. There are many ways that God speaks to us. I think this was one of those ways that God was telling me that he had more in store for me than this grand slam—something connected with my

Baptism. At the time, I didn't grasp that the grand slam would be the crowning moment of my baseball career. I thought there were going to be many more moments like it in the future. God was preparing me for something else, but at that time I had no idea what that was going to be.

Even though the College World Series occurred the week after the tournament of my life, I was no longer in the zone. The ball looked like a pea. My first at bat in the first game against our SEC rival Georgia, I hit into a double play, and all my confidence was instantly gone. I felt it switch too. It's amazing how quickly it can turn. When I was hot, it seemed like nobody was in the field—just the pitcher and me. And if I hit the ball anywhere, it was going to find a hole. When we got to the World Series, it felt like there were forty guys on the field. I knew that no matter where I hit the ball, it was going to get caught. Hitting is so psychological. I got only one hit in three games and made a couple errors.

We lost the first game against Georgia, the eventual champion. The second game we beat Georgia Southern, scoring a College World Series record 11 runs in the first inning. We lost our final game against the Stanford Cardinal 6–2.

During the College World Series, the MLB was holding the draft. I assumed that since I'd come off the tournament of my life as the MVP, I was going to get drafted. I had planned my life for that day. Nearly the whole starting lineup of Mississippi State got drafted. Several of my teammates received a phone call saying, "Congratulations, you have been drafted!" My phone stayed silent. I thought, "Well, maybe they don't have my phone number. There has to be some mistake."

Dad talked to a couple scouts after the draft, and one of them said, "Well, he is such a good student, we didn't think he wanted to pursue baseball." I was crushed. We had lost the College World Series, and I also had to face the fact that I would not be playing professional baseball. Everything I had planned for and everything that I had dreamed about was over in a flash.

I came home to Joliet feeling sorry for myself. I went into a slight depression and lost the motivation to do anything. About two weeks later though, I received a phone call from my former high school coach Jaime Garcia, who had become a coach in the Chicago White Sox system. He said, "Burke, we've had some injuries in the Minor Leagues. We are looking for a middle infielder. Tonight, we are having a tryout in South Bend, Indiana. Our general manager and some Major League scouts will be there. You should go!" Excitement built within me. Maybe the dream was not over after all! I called Joe Rodeghero and asked if he wanted to take a road trip to South Bend. He agreed, and within thirty minutes we were on the road toward Notre Dame.

There were only four guys invited to this private tryout. It could not have gone any better. They had us take ground balls from shortstop, watched us throw across the diamond, and then watched us take batting practice. At the end of the evening, they told us, "We will call you tomorrow with the news." Even though I was nervous, I felt confident because I had shown them all that I could do on the field, and I had an "in" with Coach Garcia.

Sure enough, the next day the Sox called me with the good news that I was offered a contract and that I should pack my bags to leave for Utica, New York, the next day to play in the New York–Penn League. There was very little money involved, but I didn't care. The dream was still alive! I excitedly packed my bags and prepared myself for the trip to New York.

I arrived at Utica late the next night. No one was waiting for me at the airport, so I took a cab to the hotel. This was not college baseball any longer. We were treated so well at MSU, and I had to realize that things were going to be different. I didn't know the schedule for the next day, where I was supposed to report, or the coach's phone number. I went to bed with a very uneasy feeling in my stomach. I was awakened sometime during the night with a phone call from someone from the Utica team. He had been drinking and he very angrily told me what time to report the next day. I couldn't help but think, "Wow, is this what professional baseball is all about?"

The whole Utica experience was not a positive one. In fact, it was a big disappointment. There were a lot of misunderstandings, so I talked to Coach Garcia, my parents, and Joe. All of them said to come home, that it wasn't a good situation. They said they would find me another team within the Sox organization. That didn't happen. It was a very difficult six months, but I was determined to keep working toward the dream.

Though it didn't work out well with the White Sox, I decided to give baseball one more try. I knew that I had what it takes to make it to the Major Leagues. Sometimes there are roadblocks in our path, and we must find a way to overcome them. That winter I decided to work my tail off, lift weights, run, hit, and get ready for spring training the next year. My friend Russ McNickle coached college baseball in Ocala, Florida. I went down there to work out with him for a few weeks leading up to spring training.

I went to spring training without any solid contacts. I had tryouts that went well, including one for the Pirates and one for the Indians, but none of them offered me a contract. I was devastated. I gave it my best shot, but it wasn't going to work out. It took a while to swallow that bitter pill. Everything had pointed to Major League Baseball. Everything. I finally had to face the fact that the dream was over.

CHAPTER FOUR

A DIVIDED HEART

Everyone experiences moments in their lives that make them pause and think, "How did I end up here? What led me to this?" I came back from spring training and fell into that way of thinking. What did life have for me now? Baseball was all I ever wanted to do. It was who I was. It was who I had been my entire life. Burke the Baseball Player. It had always been set in my mind and that of my friends and family that I would play baseball, work in baseball, and live my life around baseball. Why couldn't I make it? Did I do something wrong? Where was God in all of this?

My identity was shaken, and I slipped into a slight depression. I spent the rest of the spring season coaching high school baseball with Joe Rodeghero, who had become a teacher and coach at Joliet Catholic Academy. I spent this time trying to figure out my new life plan. Was I called to be a teacher and coach? Should I make another comeback with an independent team? What was God's plan for me? When I lost a game in high school or college, I had to make a conscious decision to put the loss behind me. Each game was a new start, a new chapter, where I would put the past behind me and look ahead to new opportunities. Baseball had taught me so much about life. It was time to turn the page and begin again. It was time to start a new chapter in my life.

One morning, Mom put a *USA TODAY* in front of me. The headline read, "Top Ten Jobs in the United States." I had never heard of the top job listed: actuary. I read the article. It said that actuarial science jobs were for math majors and offered high pay and low stress. It wasn't baseball, but I thought to myself, "This is what I want to do now. If I could make a lot of money with low stress, sign me up." I always loved math, and I thought this would be a good opportunity. I realized that my calling was not to be a teacher and coach, so maybe this was the way God was going to use my mathematical abilities.

I looked for actuarial positions in Illinois and found that Kemper Insurance in Long Grove had an opening. I already had the degree and didn't have to get more education, which was great because I was tired of school. Instead, I had to study for a series of ten exams that actuaries take while working. With every exam you pass, you get a pay increase. When you pass all ten exams, you become a part of something like a fellowship of actuaries, or you can become a partner. It was a promising career, so I applied for the job at Kemper, and I got it.

I started working there in the summer of 1991. It was a good job. I got to do something with my degree and to work with numbers. I commuted from Joliet to Long Grove, which was at least an hour and fifteen minutes if the traffic was good. I lived with my parents to save money. I thought if I liked the job, I would eventually buy a place near the office after I had saved some money.

I was working at Kemper only a couple weeks when I got a call from my friend Rick Kurth. He was an attorney and the president of the Danville Dans, a team in the Central Illinois Collegiate League in Danville, Illinois. I had played for the Dans for the summer of 1989 and lived with the Kurth family. "They are filming a movie about Babe Ruth here in Danville," Rick told me. "It's called *The Babe*. John Goodman is playing Babe Ruth, and they are looking for extra players on the field during filming. I am in charge of getting the players. Are you in?"

I couldn't believe it. Maybe this was my way back into a life with baseball. Despite the fact that I had only been working at Kemper for two weeks, I couldn't let this opportunity pass. I went to my boss, Dan, who fortunately for me was a baseball fan. I explained the opportunity to him, and he told me that I had to go. He gave me two weeks of vacation for my involvement in this movie.

I went to Danville and had a great experience. I was one of the extra players in the field, and I sat next to John Goodman in the dugout for a few scenes. I was the only one besides Lou Gehrig and Babe Ruth to get a hit in the movie. My godfather Joe and Mike Hutcheon, one of my college coaches and a good friend, were also in the movie. It was fun being around these men and baseball again. Some of the actors, like Bruce Boxleitner, who played Jumpin' Joe Dugan, and Richard Tyson, who played Guy Bush, would play catch with us and talk baseball during the breaks. It was great fun!

Honestly, I enjoyed working on the movie, but it was a lot of standing around as they did take after take on certain shots. It would take the whole day to film a five-minute scene. During one of the shoots, I had to slide into second base eighteen times because they were looking for the perfect take of the slide and tag. By the end of the day, I had a big strawberry on my leg. This scene made the final cut of the movie when Babe Ruth was trying to break in as a manager and coach. After two weeks of filming in Danville, it was time to get back to work as an actuary.

At Kemper, I realized early on that I worked with some good people in a good work environment. However, I found myself being bored and not looking forward to going to work. I loved numbers, but not enough to sit at a computer all day. About ten months into the job, I had a heart-to-heart conversation with Mom and Dad.

"If this is what the next forty or fifty years of my life are like," I said to them, "I don't want any part of it. I'm bored. I need something else."

Dad, always very practical, tried to talk me out of leaving. "If you plan on getting married like your brothers," he said, "this is good money. You'd be crazy to give this up. You need to make a good living to raise a family." He was right. He had given his whole life working challenging manual labor jobs to support his mom, his wife, and his boys.

Mom took the other side. "Burke," she said, "you're going to work the rest of your life. Do something you enjoy."

This was one of the best pieces of advice I had ever received. I quit my job with Kemper shortly after that conversation. Why delay quitting when I knew it wasn't the right thing for me? I certainly was not enjoying this job and knew in my heart I was made to do something else, but I didn't know what that was.

The summer of 1992 approached, and I needed to figure out what I was going to do. About that time, one of my friends and mentors from Mississippi State, Dr. David Boles, called and wanted to know how I was doing in the actuary business. I told him my heart wasn't in the work, and we talked about different career options. Hearing my desires and knowing my talents, he mentioned that I could make a career in the management side of sports. He said I could become a general manager of a Major League Baseball team. He told me to look at Ohio University, which had the first and the best graduate program in sports management. This caught my attention. A career in sports management combined two of my passions: baseball and people. I was no longer a shy teenager; I had become comfortable in my own skin, and I loved working with people. Maybe this was what I had been looking for and what God had prepared for me.

It was near the deadline for applications for graduate school at Ohio University, and they only accepted about twenty people each year. I applied and was accepted at the last minute. It was a one-year master's program, including an internship. I packed my bags and moved to Athens, Ohio, to start this new adventure to become a Major League general manager. I loved the classes and made a lot of good friends there. A lot of young men and women who had just played Division 1 sports were in the program. We dominated the co-ed intramural sports, especially softball and flag football.

I took classes at Ohio University from August until February, and then I worked a three-month internship to finish the program. Ironically, I applied and was accepted as an intern with the White Sox in Sarasota, Florida, the same team that had given me a chance to play professional baseball. That spring training, the Sox gave me many different opportunities to experience the business side of baseball. Although I loved this internship, something inside of me wasn't settled, and I didn't know what it was.

I graduated from the sports management program in the spring of 1993 with a new dream, and it was crystal clear. I was going to become the general manager of a Major League team. It would be beautiful if it was the Cubs or White Sox in Chicagoland near family and friends, but I wasn't picky. I was willing to move anywhere in the country. With my new goal in place, I applied for jobs, and I got one with the Kane County Cougars in Geneva, Illinois. When I interviewed, I had no idea that you had to start at the bottom. Like the players, you had to start at the lowest level and work your way to the top. I worked for very little money because the market was saturated with people who wanted to work in professional sports. You had to get your foot in the door and prove that you had just what it takes to move up the ladder.

The team offered me a position in the ticket office, and I accepted the offer. My friends and former elementary school teachers, Kevin and Mart O'Connor, lived close to the field. They let me stay in the room in their basement to save money while I got my feet underneath me in this new job. I started as a ticket agent and, sure enough, just as it had been while working on the movie, I loved being around baseball again. We worked long days, starting at nine in the morning and, if there was a night game, finishing at about ten or eleven at night.

In the Minor Leagues, everyone pitches in with everything. After our work was done in the ticket office, we would help clean the stadium after the game ended. I was officially at the bottom, but I was willing to pay my dues. I'm glad I had to do all the menial tasks. My parents taught me and my brothers the importance of hard work and that no work is below us. Little by little, I started working my way up the ladder in the ticket office.

* * *

I was only living with Kevin a few months when he asked me to attend a Cursillo weekend that was being offered through the Diocese of Rockford. I had started going to Mass with him and his family every Sunday at Holy Cross in Batavia. I really liked it, and there were a lot of great people that worshiped there. When he asked me to attend the Cursillo, I said yes immediately because I had always experienced profound things on religious retreats. The Cursillo was similar to the high school Kairos retreat, but it was tailored for adults. This three-day weekend would change my life. It gave me the opportunity to go to confession for the first time in my life.

I was baptized at eighteen, which was beautiful because Baptism wiped away original sin and all my personal sins that I had committed prior to my Baptism. Since I was going to be baptized to enter the Church, Fr. Mike didn't teach me much about confession. At the time I attended the Cursillo, I was intimidated by confession. I didn't know the prayers, and I was afraid to tell someone my sins, so I had avoided this sacrament.

"I know you haven't been to confession, but there is this young priest coming in," Kevin said, knowing how afraid I was to go. "He doesn't speak English really well, but he'll walk you through it."

I was nervous, but I somehow stayed in the line for confession. When it was my turn, I was shaking. My hands were sweating, and I thought my mind would go blank. The priest was so reassuring and pastoral. He gently walked me through the process. For the first time in my life, I named my sins out loud. For the first time in my life, I heard, "I absolve you from your sins in the name of the Father, and of the Son, and of the Holy Spirit." And for the first time in my life, I truly felt forgiven.

My parents always encouraged our family to confess our sins straight to God, and I knew God could forgive sins anywhere. God is bigger than a confessional, and he can do anything. But I had learned an important lesson about the sacrament. As a human being, I needed to say these things out loud, and I needed to hear "I absolve you from your sins." The priest represents Christ here on earth. It was such a cleansing moment for me, and I walked out of the confessional and the weekend feeling light and free. I vowed to myself to make confession a regular part of my spiritual life.

After the Cursillo, I felt inspired to go to daily Mass for the first time in my life, and I was learning about the power of God's grace in the Eucharist. There was this fire in me to become a better disciple of Christ and to spend more time with him. The first week of going to Mass every day, I noticed one of the ladies who was always there watching me.

"Burke, be careful," she said to me after Mass one day.

"What do you mean 'Be careful'?" I asked.

"Well, that's how my son got started," she said, nodding her head. "Going to daily Mass."

"What do you mean?"

She looked at me with a smile and said, "He's a priest today."

Fr. Max Striedl, her son, started to go to daily Mass after his Cursillo, and it helped him discern to enter the seminary and become a priest. She was pointing out to me the power of daily Mass. Her words planted the seed of the priesthood in my mind, and it would surface at different times in the coming months and years. When it did, I would remind myself that the priesthood was nowhere on my radar. I was going to be the general manager of the Cubs or White Sox, get married, make a lot of money, have a big family, and live happily ever after. Priesthood was not a part of my plan.

* * *

At this point in my life, I was developing a deeper relationship with God, who loved me and wanted to share his divine life with me. I learned that God was with me always. I was realizing that even in the most trying experiences of life, like the end of my baseball career, God was right by my side. But it takes time to build trust in any relationship, and our relationship was in its infant stages. I didn't trust God as much as I trusted myself. I'd wanted God to bless my plans in baseball. I never stopped to ask God what he wanted me to do. I was stubborn and wanted to follow my path. God was trying to show me another way, but I had not opened my heart to follow him yet.

God was patient with me. He pursued me like the Hound of Heaven in Francis Thompson's famous poem, but he respected my freedom. He was inviting me to a deeper place that I was not yet willing to go.

By 1994 and the start of my second year with the Kane County Cougars, I became the ticket manager, and they increased my pay. I was making a livable wage and was able to move out of Kevin and Mart's basement and get my own apartment, which ironically was a renovated convent. Living in that convent was not the greatest experience; it felt sterile and not at all like home.

Everyone assumed that I would get married, including Kevin and Mart. After Mass one day, they introduced me to Stephanie Emmons, who was a beautiful girl inside and out. We started a friendship and then began dating. On our first date, I took her to the cinema to see *Schindler's List*, which was not a good idea. We walked out of the theater in stunned silence, with Stephanie wiping her tear-stained face. I figured that after my blunder of

PHOTO GALLERY

1969: Me, age two.

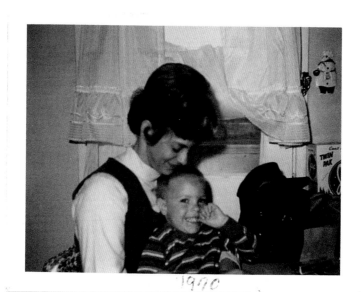

1970: With my mother, Janet, at three years old.

1971: The Masters brothers. Top to bottom: Brock, Blaine, and me.

1976: Playing for Jack's Sports team at nine years old.

1978: Age eleven, playing for the Barrett's Ace Hardware team.

1983: Sophomore year at Providence Catholic High School.

1983: Sophomore baseball picture at Providence Catholic High School.

1985: With my mother Janet after graduation from Providence Catholic High School.

MISSISSIPPI STATE BULLDOGS

BURKE MASTERS

1989: Junior year at Mississippi State University.

1990: At Brock's wedding.

1991: The Masters brothers: Blaine, Brock, and me (seated).

1990: The Academic All-American Player of the Year.

May 26, 1990: The grand slam against Florida State at Mississippi State during the regional tournament.

1990: Signing autographs on May 25, 1990.

1991: With John Goodman during the filming of *The Babe* in Danville, Illinois.

1996: The Masters Brothers: Blaine, Brock, and me (kneeling).

1997: Tod and Janet Masters (and Bud the dog), about one year before Mom passed away after battling cancer.

2002: With Cardinal Francis George at Mundelein Seminary graduation.

June 1, 2002: Ordination day.

June 1, 2002: Bishop Joseph Imesch laying hands on me during the ordination rite.

June 2, 2002: Celebrating Mass for the first time at the Cathedral of St. Raymond in Joliet, Illinois.

June 2, 2002: With Matt DiMarco and Stephanie Emmons after my first Mass.

November 23, 2002: Fr. Joel Rippinger and me with Matt and Stephanie DiMarco after their wedding. It was my second wedding as a priest.

2009: Baptism of my godchild Andrew at Holy Cross Parish in Batavia, Illinois.

2009: Playing Euchre with Blaine, Brock, and Dad.

2016: With Ray McKenna (founder of Catholic Athletes for Christ) and Joe Madden (Manager of the Chicago Cubs) during spring training.

2016: With Dr. Tom Nelson during batting practice at Wrigley Field.

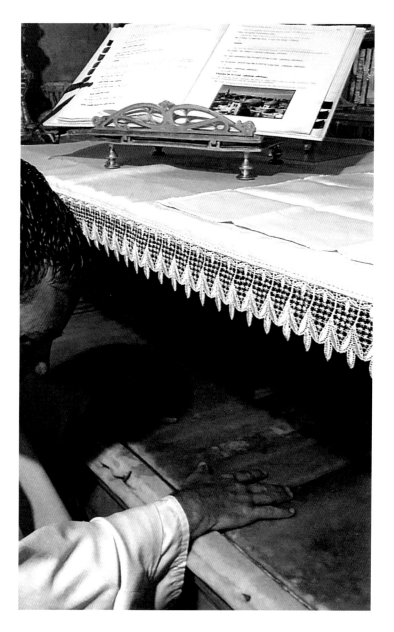

2019: Mass at the tomb of Jesus in the Church of the Holy Sepulchre.

July 2022: With Mike Sweeney at the Catholic Baseball Camp at Montini Catholic High School in Lombard, Illinois.

2022: Spring training with Mike Sweeney, recording one of my daily devotionals.

2022: In the Holy Land with Blaine, his wife Nancy, and Brock.

2022: Walking El Camino de Santiago. Left to right: Me, Joe Miller, Mark Hagen, Ed Burjek, and Rick Erwin.

picking that movie, this would be our first and last date, but Stephanie was forgiving. I redeemed myself by taking her to see *Dumb and Dumber* on our next date. It was so easy and fun to be around her, and we both started picturing a future together.

"Let's stop by church," Stephanie said one night while we were out for dinner.

"What's going on at church?" I asked.

"They have Eucharistic Adoration on Tuesdays," she said.

I had been Catholic about ten years by this time, but I had never heard of Eucharistic Adoration. When I asked her what we were going to experience, she explained, "We're going to spend an hour in silent prayer in front of Jesus in the Blessed Sacrament."

It all sounded good, but there was one problem: I was afraid of silence. Who do we encounter in the silence? Ourselves and God. I was constantly afraid of what God was going to tell me. Even with receiving the sacrament of Reconciliation, I didn't like the person I was. I knew I wasn't living the way God wanted me to live, so I never really slowed down long enough to listen to God's voice. I kept myself busy so that I didn't have to face myself either. But since Stephanie had just invited me into that silence, I couldn't refuse. I would have to face both God and myself.

The first night we went to Adoration, I didn't know how to pray. I just read a book. It was a good religious book, but I didn't know how to communicate with God. When we walked out, she said, "That was great, wasn't it? We should go back next week!" I wasn't jumping for joy at the idea, but I wanted to be with Stephanie, so I agreed that this would be a weekly date for us. We went to Adoration for an hour every Tuesday. Little by little, I put the book down and began to talk to God. Eventually, I craved the hour because it was filled with so much peace. Each week I started looking forward to going to Adoration.

After a few months of going to Adoration, the idea of priesthood came to mind each time I prayed. It was not voluntary. The image of me celebrating Mass would pop into my mind, and I couldn't ignore it. I'd say, "God, if that's you, you have to make this clear because I do not want to be a priest." In the weeks after that prayer, random people came up to me and said, "You know, Burke, I think you'd make a good priest." And after Mass one Sunday, I was lost in my own thoughts about the priesthood when a lady walked up to me and said, "You're going to be a priest one day." Then she just walked away. I have never seen her before or since. Whether it was an angel or just someone sent by God, I thought, "Oh my gosh! Oh God, I think I know what you want, but I still don't want to do it." I pictured priesthood as a boring and sterile lifestyle. I couldn't understand why God would call me to do something that would make me miserable.

Everything that I had heard about God was that he was good. People told me that God had a great plan for my life. I could not understand how a good God did not allow me to reach the Major Leagues. Now he was asking me to give up Stephanie and a career in the management side of baseball. I thought I knew what would make me happy, and priesthood was not it. I had no idea of the great plans God had in store for me. God kept teaching me how to trust him. I often feel like God is my Father and I am a little boy. He takes me by the hand and tells me, "Follow me. You can trust me."

Stephanie was a wonderful person and would make an amazing wife and mother. Everything, every part of who she was, was perfect for me. If I listed characteristics that I looked for in a future spouse, Stephanie had all of them. She wasn't a big baseball fan, but she was willing to learn. If I was ever going to marry someone, it would be her. And yet there was something missing. Something was holding me back from her and from our future together. And I figured out what it was: the thought of the priesthood became too hard to ignore. I had to face the fact that maybe God was calling me to become a priest.

We had been dating for almost a year when I told her what I had been sensing. Stephanie was quiet as she took time to consider what I shared. "If this is your call from God," she finally said, "you have to follow it. I can't compete with God. If this is your vocation, you have to follow God's call."

Stephanie showed me why I cared about her so deeply. She was a selfless woman of faith. We decided to break up and go our separate ways so that I could discern the priesthood. I said, "Okay God, if this is what you want me to do, I'll do it, but I have my doubts." I was still afraid to trust God, so I didn't go running to the seminary right away.

I was suffering from a problem that many young people face: I was of two minds. On one hand, I was hearing God's invitation, and on the other, I was reluctant to accept it. I didn't trust God enough to surrender to his will.

I needed to grow closer to God to see if this call was legitimate. I got involved in the Cursillo movement, and at my parish I became a lector and a Eucharistic minister. I volunteered to help with the Rite of Christian Initiation of Adults. RCIA included weekly classes to help people learn more about the Catholic faith before joining the Church. I had to admit that I felt comfortable when I was at church, but I never thought that it would be my home one day. I avoided the thought of the priesthood when I could. I stubbornly held out from applying to the seminary because I was in a spiritual tug of war with God.

One of the nights I was helping with RCIA at the church, in walked a guy wearing a Mississippi State baseball hat. Matt DiMarco was a young adult in his twenties, a baptized Catholic who had never received the sacrament of Confirmation. I had to find out why someone in Illinois was wearing an MSU baseball hat. It turned out that he had a great friend who studied at MSU and was in the golf management program there. We talked several hours that evening and became instant friends. He started to come to the RCIA classes. His mother died when he was only two years old, and he never completed his sacraments. He asked me to be his sponsor for Confirmation. It was an honor to help him enter more fully into the Church. I could tell it was part of God's plan that we became friends.

* * *

In 1995, Matt and I rented a place together in Chicago near Wrigley Field. Matt was a pilot and flew a lot, and the apartment was not too far from O'Hare Airport. I was commuting to work with the Kane County Cougars in the suburbs. Neither of us was home very much at the same time. Stephanie and I had stayed friends after we broke up, and we would talk from time to time. I introduced Matt to her, and the three of us would occasionally go out together.

Halfway through 1996, I still hadn't applied for seminary. I had ignored the call and had even tried to date again. I thought to myself that maybe it was just the fact that Stephanie and I were not right for each other. Maybe I would find someone else and that nudge toward the priesthood would go away. I dated a girl for a few months and had the same feeling that I got with Stephanie. Although she was another wonderful, faithful Catholic woman, something was missing. The thought of the priesthood would not leave me alone.

After you attend a men's Cursillo as a candidate, you can go back on subsequent retreats, be a part of the team, and give talks. I served on the team for several Cursillo weekends. I found that I really loved giving talks, being with these faithful men, and helping others grow closer to Christ. In the fall of 1996, I was speaking at a Cursillo and feeling the power of the Holy Spirit. The closing Mass at the end of the retreat was celebrated by a priest I had never met. While I knelt for the consecration, I thought, "God, I know you want me to be a priest, but, boy, I don't want to do it. This isn't part of my plans. You have to make it absolutely clear if you want me to do this." As I was praying, I opened my eyes to look for a sign. Nothing had changed around me, but the priest was looking right at me. I thought, "Oh man, lightning is going to strike or something." I waited, but nothing supernatural happened. Mass finished as normal, and I breathed a sigh of relief. I was off the hook.

After Mass, I was helping clean the retreat center before going home. I was taking some chairs down the stairs, and I ran right into the priest. He was obviously looking for me, but he seemed uncomfortable and a little embarrassed. We chatted for a while, but I could tell there was something more on his mind.

"Father," I said, "it seems like you came over here for a reason. Is there something you wanted to tell me?"

"Uh, well, this might sound crazy," he said. "I don't know what your situation is in life, whether you are dating someone or married . . . but I felt that when our eyes met during Mass, God was asking me to ask you to be a priest."

The hair on the back of my neck stood up. The moment our eyes met at Mass was the exact moment I had been asking for the sign. I don't always share that story because sometimes people think that they must have that kind of dramatic sign to know whether God is calling them or not. I believe you don't need huge signs if you're listening to God and are open to his will. As I look back on my life, God was speaking to me many times along the way. I just didn't want to listen. He had to pull out a two-by-four to hit me across the head. It was the final straw that broke my stubbornness, and I surrendered to God that night. When the priest said those words to me, I felt peace. I knew that this was what God wanted me to do. I told my friend Kevin on the way home from the retreat what happened and that I had to give seminary a try. He was overjoyed at the news!

Despite the signs that I received, I still wavered between being sure of my vocation and having severe doubts. I thought that I would go to seminary for a year and wouldn't like it. I could get God off my back and return to my plans. I had it all figured out.

Around that same time, I had made good contacts in the baseball world. Like in anything, it's not so much what you know but who you know. I knew the general manager for the Florida Marlins. We were in conversation about a position in the front office in Miami, which is what I had been working toward. My former college roommate, Bo McKinnis, had become an agent for Major League Baseball players. He was looking for a guy who was good with numbers and who could manage contracts and statistics. Both guys came to me with these perfect opportunities to continue a career in baseball at the same time I was feeling this call to seminary.

"God," I thought, "you're placing these dream jobs in my lap, but you're calling me to the priesthood?" It wasn't as if I had nothing better to do and just thought "Oh well, might as well just go to the seminary." There were a lot of good opportunities out there. As I prayed and thought about it, I realized that God just wanted me to know that I was free to choose. I could choose any of these paths, and he would respect my freedom. I could choose to stay in baseball, or I could follow this calling to the priesthood. I continued to pray and think about it, and in the end, I knew that if I didn't go to seminary, I was always going to wonder "What if?" I figured that if I went to seminary and decided it was not for me, these other job offers or something similar would still be available. I made plans to go to seminary in the fall of 1997. I had to get this thought of priesthood out of my head, one way or another.

CHAPTER FIVE

THE GIFT OF THE RED BIRD

I didn't know how to apply to the seminary, so I went to Fr. Steven St. Jules, the pastor of Holy Cross Parish in Batavia, Illinois. He put me in contact with the vocation director in the Diocese of Rockford, and I started the interview process. Before I knew it, I was a seminarian.

An excitement that I had not experienced began to well up within me. The diocese sent me to the University of St. Mary of the Lake, commonly known as Mundelein Seminary, a beautiful place located a little northwest of Chicago. Built around a picturesque lake and surrounded by trees, the campus invited me in with all the other first-year seminarians. On my first day, I met Dennis Spies, a farm boy from the Diocese of Joliet. Although he was much more outgoing than I was, and we were very different in many ways, we became friends right away.

The atmosphere at Mundelein was different from any other I had experienced. Every one of the seminarians was there to help and encourage one another, and the brotherhood among the seminarians, faculty, and staff was strong. We were not there to compete with one another, as you might find in many university settings. Instead, we looked to help each other grow. From the moment I stepped across the threshold of the seminary dorm, deep down I knew I was going to stay. I was overcome with peace and the sense that this was where I was supposed to be. Finally, I knew where I belonged and what I was called to do. Gone were the anger and disappointment I had experienced when my Major League dreams had been crushed. All my doubts, all my talk of only staying for a year to "get God off my back," were gone. I had listened to him. This was the beginning of my learning how to follow God's will for my life. He replaced my fear, worry, and anger with trust, peace, and joy.

For men who had four-year college degrees, seminary at that time was a five-year process: one year of philosophy or pre-the-ology, then four years of theology. Now the Church requires two years of philosophy, for a total of six years for college graduates who enter seminary. We had twenty-four men in my class when we started philosophy. Coming from a math background, studying philosophy was a challenge for me. We were learning how to reason and how to write. I was used to the "Give me a problem and I'll solve it" method, but after we began to study philosophy, I realized how important it was. They say philosophy is the handmaid to theology: it teaches you how to think and prepares you for the study of God.

In addition to Dennis, another of my good friends was Dave Hoefler from the Diocese of Springfield, Illinois. We had a lot of fun together, and both Dennis and Dave became like my brothers. My blood brothers, Brock and Blaine, had moved out to Colorado and started families. They both supported my decision to enter seminary. According to Brock, it wasn't a surprise I wanted to be a priest. My brothers saw that I was happy, so even though they weren't Catholic, they were happy for me.

In October 1997, during my first fall semester, my parents came to Mundelein for a family weekend. I showed them all around campus and told them how glad I was to be there. Mom wasn't feeling well. She complained of tingling in her arms and hands, and she couldn't walk very far without needing a break. Normally, she was very active and always on the go. After all, she had kept up with three boys for many years! Now, she was exhausted just walking short distances around the seminary. It wasn't like her, but she tried to not draw any attention away from me during this visit.

She and Dad were both very proud parents and supportive of me. Two of my classmates were also converts to Catholicism, but neither of them became priests. A major factor in their leaving the seminary was that their families did not support their decision. One was told by his parents, "It is either priesthood or us. You choose." I was so thankful that my parents never gave me that ultimatum. Knowing that I had my parents' support gave me great peace and joy. Every day I was growing in confidence in my vocation as a priest, and I was learning to trust God.

Mundelein was, and still is, a community based on encouragement and brotherhood. One of my biggest fears going to seminary was that I would not have anything in common with my classmates. What I found was that there were not only plenty of guys who loved sports but also some who had been Division 1 athletes in college. We played basketball regularly at the seminary. I started a baseball team as well. It was fun and competitive but not cutthroat.

We also supported each other academically. For example, I did better studying by myself, but I saw that Dennis, a big extrovert, struggled with studying solo. Dennis' potential as a priest was evident. He was intelligent, compassionate, and his love for God and his people was deep. He just had trouble studying alone. We came up with a system where I would have time to study on my own, but then we'd get a group together to talk about our lessons. This allowed the extroverts to study out loud and gave me the opportunity to teach what I had been learning. We all excelled by using the gifts God had given us.

* * *

I had only been in the seminary a few months when one day I heard a knock at my door. My room was at the end of a hallway, leading into a social hall, where a lot of traffic passed, and it was common for friends to drop in. I opened the door and there was Bishop Kaffer, the Auxiliary Bishop of the Diocese of Joliet. I was so surprised! He had been my high school principal at Providence before he became a bishop. I had respected him greatly. He had been a big influence on me in high school. One of the reasons that Catholicism attracted me was his positive and energetic faith.

"I didn't know you were in the seminary!" he exclaimed.

"Yes," I said, feeling a bit embarrassed. "I'm sorry I forgot to tell you!"

He laughed and said that he was at the seminary visiting the Joliet seminarians and was overjoyed that I was discerning the call to be a priest. "What are you doing studying for the Diocese of Rockford?" he asked.

"I don't know," I said. I explained that I had moved to Batavia and felt the first inkling of a call to the priesthood at Adoration and on a Cursillo. "I discerned my vocation," I said, "and before I knew it, I was studying for Rockford. I did not know how the process worked, but after meeting with the vocation director a few times, I felt more and more confident that I should enter the seminary. I did not even think about going back to my home diocese of Joliet."

He said, "I would have thought that growing up in Joliet, you would have come back there, but I am so proud of you, and I will be praying for your vocation."

After our conversation, I began wondering, "Why am I studying for Rockford?" I had grown up in the Diocese of Joliet, only ten minutes from the Cathedral of St. Raymond. Since entering the seminary, I had gone with Rockford seminarians to events in the diocese. And although they were good men and friends, I did not feel that I belonged there. I started thinking about transferring to Joliet. It seemed that the Holy Spirit was calling me back home.

What I did not know was that something unexpected was about to call me back to Joliet.

In May 1998, about a week before finishing my first year of seminary, Dad called. We were entering finals week. I do not remember the day, but I remember his voice. It was somber, and Dad was not a phone person. I knew something was amiss.

"I need you to come home," he said. "We just found out that your mother has been diagnosed with stage-four lung cancer."

I spoke to Fr. Canary, the rector of the seminary, right away. He said, "Go home and take care of your family. Your grades are fine, so don't worry about your classes. You don't have to take the finals."

What an amazing response from the seminary! They were practicing what they preached, putting the priorities where they needed to be in this situation. I gathered my things quickly and went home.

Mom probably had the cancer for a while, but it was just now being diagnosed. It had started in her lungs and had spread to her liver and brain. The doctors were very concerned. I didn't need a medical degree to know that this was very serious. They gave us options but recommended that we choose an aggressive chemotherapy for Mom because the cancer was spreading fast. We opted for a powerful experimental chemotherapy, and they started right away. Every day was critical in this process. I took her to all her chemotherapy and doctor's appointments so that Dad could continue working. Sitting with her during chemo treatments, we had lots of time to talk. She slept a lot during the treatments as well as when we'd get home. The chemotherapy wiped her out, but I treasured all of those conversations we were able to have when she was awake.

My brothers and their families came from Colorado to visit with Mom in the weeks following the diagnosis. Brock had three children and Blaine had two, and the five grandchildren made their grandmother smile. We were getting good news with each doctor's visit. The new scans were showing that the tumors were shrinking. Our entire family was cautiously optimistic.

While I was home in Joliet, I made an appointment with Bishop Doran, the Bishop of Rockford, and told him that I wanted to transfer to the Joliet diocese. I explained that my mom had cancer and I wanted to be close to her and my dad. The conversation didn't go the way I thought it would. He said that he thought I was making an emotional decision, so he wasn't going to let me transfer. I didn't know how everything worked, and I wanted to do things the right way. Over the next few weeks, I talked to some priests who told me that I was not canonically tied to the Diocese of Rockford. I wanted to follow Church protocol, but I felt strongly that the Holy Spirit was calling me back to Joliet.

Mom and I went to the doctor for another scan. We got good news. They said that the tumors were the smallest they had been yet. It was July 7, 1998, and we went to Wendy's to have a burger to celebrate the good news. When we came home, she went out on the back porch. She sat there for a while looking out over the cornfield without really seeing it. There was something there that I hadn't seen in her before. I asked her if she was okay, and she just said something under her breath like "Yeah, I'm okay."

I wonder if she knew what was coming. My mother was a doer and was always in the middle of the activity. As I look back on it, the way she stared into the cornfield that day tells me she expected something bad was going to happen. She just wasn't herself. Despite the good news of the day, she wasn't celebrating.

After dinner, Mom, Dad, and I sat in the living room, watching the MLB All-Star game. She was tired, so at about nine o'clock she went to bed in the next room, and Dad and I continued watching the game. Then we heard her coughing. The doctors had told us that the chemotherapy was working on the tumors. They said not to panic if she coughs or if she spits up some of the tumor. She didn't just cough once though; it persisted. I thought this might be a good thing. Maybe she could get rid of some of the tumor.

She got out of bed and entered the living room where we were, and we saw that it wasn't good. It wasn't just gunk from her lungs. There was blood—a lot of it. The room turned into pure chaos. I got her to the bathroom; Dad ran to the phone to call 911. As she was coughing, she mouthed the words "I can't breathe" before she passed out. I caught her as her body went limp. Holding Mom there on the bathroom floor, I felt the life leaving her body. Dad was talking to the emergency technicians on the phone, and he relayed to me instructions on how to perform CPR. I tried to do everything they said, but there was so much blood and chaos. It was awful.

It seemed like an eternity, but the paramedics arrived within ten to fifteen minutes. I stepped back and they started working on her. I knew. I knew she was gone. I could tell that she wasn't coming back. It was a surreal moment. They were working on her in the bathroom, and Dad and I were standing in the living room, stunned. As this horrific scene unfolded, I looked around. I saw her purse on the kitchen counter. I looked out the window in the living room and saw her car in the driveway. It was like time stopped. She was going to God, and all those material things stayed behind.

I envisioned my mother coming face-to-face with God. I don't think he was asking her, "What kind of car did you drive? How much money did you make?" He was asking her the fundamental question: "How much did you love?" Suddenly my life flashed before my eyes. All the memories of Mom loving my brothers and me streamed before me. My mother taught me what love is all about: laying down your life for a friend. Throughout her life, Mom was teaching us one of the most important Scripture passages. When Jesus was asked which commandment is the greatest, he said, "Love the Lord your God with all your heart, and with all your soul, and with all your mind," and "Love your neighbor as yourself" (Matt. 22:37–38). Mom, by word and example, taught us that there is nothing more important in life than our relationships with God and others. Jesus said, "No one has greater love than this, to lay down one's life for one's friends" (John 15:13). My mother lived out this passage daily.

The paramedics did what they could at the house. They were still working on her as they lifted her on the gurney and put her in the ambulance. It must have been around 9:30 p.m., but everything was a blur. My Uncle Terry and Aunt Judi came over from across the street in shock. They said they'd follow us to the hospital. Dad and I got in the car in complete silence. I couldn't say anything, and neither could he. We followed the ambulance to the hospital, where they had us wait in a small, white room. It was not long before they came out and told us that they were unable to save her.

"Do you want to go in to see her and say goodbye?" they asked.

"Yes," I said.

Walking into the room was hard. It hit me that when the soul leaves the body, the body is different. What we saw in that hospital room was just a body. It wasn't my mom. Although we were saying goodbye to her, I knew that she wasn't there. In a way, this sensation made it easier because I was thinking that she was with God already. We said our goodbyes, kissed her, and went home. I could not believe what had just transpired that evening.

I knew my life had suddenly changed in a matter of minutes; I didn't know how to react. Even though she had cancer, we had not allowed ourselves to think about death. We had remained positive and believed without a doubt that she would beat it. She was only fifty-seven years old. We figured her body could withstand the treatment. The medical reports had gotten better day by day, and then, suddenly, she was gone.

When Dad and I got home from the hospital, we were unable to say anything. We were men of few words anyway, but it was very difficult for us to talk about the feelings we were experiencing that night. The smell of bleach stung my nose when we entered the house. Terry and Judi had cleaned up. They didn't want us coming home to that scene. They were close to Mom, and I can only imagine how hard it was on them to clean up her blood. Dad and I said good night, but it was going to be one of the worst nights of our lives. I didn't sleep a minute. I curled up in bed in the fetal position as I tried to comprehend all that had happened. I replayed the events of the evening. I recalled how my brothers responded when they received the call that Mom had died. Everyone was in total shock.

This night was going to haunt me forever. My memory pushed up random thoughts about Mom: her contagious laugh, her kind disposition, her willingness to help anyone, her gift of listening that led many to confide in her, her welcoming everyone, making them feel like they were the only people in the world at that moment. While she chatted with unexpected visitors to our home, she would create an amazing meal; the food would just appear on the table. She was so engaged in the conversation, no one noticed that she had been cooking. As the youngest, I was especially close to her. We talked about anything and everything. She never judged me. That's not to say she never disciplined me, but I know that she loved me unconditionally. The darkness of this night would overwhelm the joyful memories I had of my mother for some time.

* * *

The next morning was such a beautiful July day, but I hated it. I felt like someone had been kicking me in the stomach all night. I was in such intense physical pain. It's amazing how much spiritual and emotional pain can manifest themselves physically. Standing on the deck, where my mother had looked out over the cornfield the day before, I stared blankly at the large willow tree in the backyard. I stood there crying.

"God, I just want to know that she's okay," I prayed in my despair. At that moment, a cardinal landed in the willow tree right in front of me and began to sing. My mom, a huge St. Louis Cardinals fan, decorated the house with little cardinal figurines everywhere. Many times, we pass things off as a happy coincidence, but as I heard that bird singing brilliantly, I felt the Lord starting to calm the chaotic storm of the night before. I felt that God was saying, "It's okay; she's with me." It didn't change the fact that my mother was gone, but it gave me some consolation. Mom and Dad were good people, but they had not been churchgoers since they married. I was always concerned for their souls. I believed that God was showing me his great mercy. Despite the pain I was experiencing, God was breaking through to comfort me through his creation, his beautiful cardinal.

We started the process of planning the wake and funeral, buying a cemetery plot, and helping my brothers and other family members arrive from Colorado and elsewhere. Wakes and funerals made me uncomfortable, as I had only lost one grandparent at this point. This funeral took everything to a whole new level. It was for my mother, the person I loved most in the world. I was nervous because I didn't know how I would handle my emotions. After I experienced the wake, I understood why we have them. We counted over a thousand friends and family in the guest book who had come to pay their respects for my mother and share condolences with our family.

I was overwhelmed to see the brotherhood of the priesthood at the wake. One by one, my seminarian brothers and priests from Rockford and Joliet filed in. There must have been at least fifty of them. The Rockford priests, who I'd come to know, and the Joliet priests, who I hardly knew, all came to this nondenominational wake for the mother of a new seminarian. It brought our family much comfort during our greatest tragedy. One of Mom's good friends, Kay Collins, was a chaplain at Silver Cross Hospital, where Mom had worked. She had known Mom for years, and she officiated a touching service at the wake. The amount of kindness and love poured out that day in memory of my mom was beautiful and something I will never forget.

The next day the service at the funeral home was a blur. The only thing I remember were my friends Dennis and Dave coming to support me. I recall the graveside service clearly. As we stood there, I wondered if something would happen. I just wanted to see something assuring. I hoped to see angels or her soul rising or just anything, but all I saw was her body going into the ground. What if there was no life after death? What if all I believed was wrong? These questions raced through my mind and led me into a real crisis of faith. If I did not believe, I knew I needed to leave the seminary. I prayed that God would show me a sign or give me a reason to continue this journey toward priesthood.

As I looked down on her casket, I reflected on what I had learned the night before about Mom and what she thought about my call. At the wake, I talked to some of her friends from the hospital. "You know Burke," they said, "we've been following your baseball career through your mom all these years. And we'd often ask her, 'How's Burke doing in baseball?' And your mom would say, 'He's doing great, but I wouldn't be surprised if he becomes a priest.'" She was saying this to her friends long before I ever thought about going to seminary. She knew back when I was in college, when I was in grad school, when I dated Stephanie. Long before I knew my vocation, my mother saw it in me and shared it with her friends.

They said that my mom never told me because she didn't want me to feel pressure from her. She wanted me to find my path on my own. She knew that her words would influence me if she told me. Hearing this news from Mom's friends consoled me. It helped me get through the crisis of faith and vocation rather quickly. My mother cared for me in life and in death. This didn't surprise me because we were so connected at every level—spiritually, emotionally, psychologically. I believe that my mom was speaking through her friends to tell me that I was supposed to stay in the seminary. I decided to go back to the seminary that fall.

I had a little over a month before seminary started again, but all the paperwork Dad and I had to process for Mom filled the time. I had no idea how much needed to be done, like getting death certificates, canceling accounts, calling insurance companies, and changing names on documents. It was a good bonding time for Dad and me. We spent a lot of time together that month. I tried to console him as he was going through his grieving process. Dad was not doing well, having just lost the woman he had loved for forty years. He told me he'd never love anyone like he loved my mother. He also told me that he would never marry again. "Dad, never say never," I said. He was only fifty-nine years old when Mom died.

The thought of him marrying again didn't bother me. What bothered me were the recurring nightmares of that terrible night. Brock and Blaine told me they were sorry I had to go through all of that. They also told me that they were glad we were there to comfort her. Even with the nightmares, I was glad I had been there. I wouldn't have wanted her to die like that alone.

⁂

With the fall semester in sight, I went back to the Bishop of Rockford. I told him I wanted to switch to Joliet even more now that my mom had died. I said I wanted to serve the diocese in which I had been raised, and I wanted to be close to my dad. The bishop was not happy that I was back in his office just a month later with the same request. Technically, I did not need his permission, but I wanted to do things the right way. That was how my parents raised me. It was a difficult conversation, but at the end he said he would let me go. He worked out the transfer with Bishop Joseph Imesch of the Diocese of Joliet.

I went back to Mundelein in the fall, but this time as a seminarian for the Diocese of Joliet. As soon as I settled in, it hit me that I had not allowed myself to grieve. In the role of the seminarian of the family, I was trying to take care of my mom, the funeral, my dad, my brothers, and everyone else. The same perfectionism that I thought I had dealt with had resurfaced. I felt that I had to keep my guard up, bury my emotions, and serve everyone else because I was studying to be a priest. When I got to Mundelein, I could let my guard down for the first time with my brother seminarians. I didn't have to be strong around them.

What I found was not sadness that had built up in me but anger, and I vented that anger to Dave and Dennis. Sometimes I would snap and say things to them that made me pause afterward and think, "Wow! Where did that come from?" I said some hurtful things to Dave, and I could see him pulling back. Neither he nor I understood what was happening. It had a very negative impact on our friendship. I do not blame Dave for pulling back on our friendship. I probably would have done the same thing if I were in his shoes. Sometime later I apologized, and he forgave me. We are currently working on rebuilding the friendship that was once there.

Dennis knew that my anger was not directed at him. He allowed me to vent with him and did not take it personally. "If you're angry and you need to vent," Dennis said, "bring it to me. If you are going to yell at someone, yell at me. I am your friend, and I am going to love you through it." As he allowed me to express my anger, it strengthened our relationship. He taught me a great lesson. As a priest, many people are angry at something, and they need to vent. I decided I would not take things personally even though words spoken in anger might be hurtful. Dennis understood, even though I didn't at the time, that I wasn't angry at him. I was angry with God.

I tried to work through the pain, the grief, and the anger in spiritual direction, but it was hard. My perfectionism made grieving difficult. I had a hard time admitting that I wasn't perfect. I'd get angry at myself for being angry. Good people don't get angry—this was a lie that I believed.

* * *

At another level, my second year of seminary was great. I loved the challenges of my classes, and I got to know my Joliet brother seminarians even better. I was very much at peace with my decision to switch dioceses. I grew deeper in my faith, but a part of me was not able to give myself fully to the formation process. I was not dealing with the pain of Mom's death; I ignored it. My anger was still there, and my dad was still struggling. I was able to go home and visit with him often on weekends. He was suffering and did not do well living alone. I was worried about him.

Dad had never lived on his own his whole life. He went from his family home to college, and then he married my mom. Mom cooked, cleaned, did the laundry, and did everything inside the house. Dad took care of everything outside the house. I noticed the difference in our vocations. He was meant to be married, and I was meant to be a priest. I brought my seminarian friends home on the weekends to give Dad company. They were good at lifting his spirits, and mine too.

The first summer after Mom's death, I was sent to Mexico to study Spanish in Cuernavaca. When I came back from the summer assignment, I wanted to spend a few weeks with Dad before returning to seminary. But I was sent to live in a parish to get more experience in the diocese.

Dad and I talked on the phone more since we often couldn't meet in person. He told me that he had looked for a new manager at his office and that he hired my Aunt Judi's best friend Jan. Our family had known Jan for years. After a while, Dad said that he was taking Jan out for lunch. A while after that, lunch turned into dinner. I was happy for Dad. With both my brothers out in Colorado, it was just me and him. I felt a big sense of responsibility for Dad during that first year after Mom's death, and I worried he was going to do something crazy. But when Jan came into the picture, he started living again. She gave him a purpose for living.

After some time of dating Jan, Dad asked me and my brothers for permission to get married again. I told him, "Dad that's great. You have my support." My brothers also supported him. On April 15, 2000, he and Jan got married in the Methodist church in New Lenox, Illinois, the church that Jan attended while growing up. She was a wonderful lady, and it was so good to see how her presence changed my dad's outlook. With Dad taken care of and beginning to live again, a weight I didn't know I had been carrying was lifted off my shoulders.

* * *

That summer of 2000, two years after my mom's death, I finally found what I needed: a place and the permission to grieve. Dennis and I went to the Institute for Priestly Formation (IPF) in Omaha, Nebraska, which offers an entire summer for seminarians focused on spiritual life and prayer. We started with an eight-day silent retreat where I met with my spiritual director every day. Then we had weekly spiritual direction for the rest of the summer. My spiritual director was amazing. I told him about Mom's death and the nightmares, which had lessened but were still there.

"Burke," he said, "to find healing, you've got to go back to that night."

I couldn't go back there. I didn't want to relive that night. I had been trying everything I could to avoid it for the last two years. I wanted to forget the horror of that night forever.

"Just like any wound," he continued, "if you ignore it, it's not going to heal. But if you go there with Jesus, you will find healing. I want you to go into the chapel, maybe at night when no one else is around. Go back to that night in your imagination and invite Jesus into it. Ask him, 'Lord, where were you that night?'"

Night came, and I went to the chapel. I was afraid. I did not want to do it, but I trusted my spiritual director. I went back to that night in my imagination. I felt all the emotions again as if it happened yesterday. I saw the blood, sensed the anxiety and fear. I felt Mom collapse into my arms again and felt the helplessness. I saw the bathroom floor, the blood, all of it. At that moment, I asked the Lord, "Where were you?"

The image that flooded my mind was the Pietà, Michelangelo's sculpture of Mary holding Jesus, but reversed. Instead of the mother holding the body of her lifeless son, it was the son holding the body of his lifeless mother. I held my mother in my arms just as Mary held Jesus at the foot of the cross. Jesus was there too, and he had his arms wrapped around both of us. God was dispelling the lie that I had come to believe: that Jesus had abandoned us at the hour of our greatest need. Jesus was showing me that he was with us the whole time.

I had cried only a few times in those two years. Most of the time my feelings were blocked up like a dam. I didn't allow myself to feel; it hurt so badly. That night in the chapel the floodgates opened, and the tears poured. I could feel the healing taking place. The darkness that had been in me was replaced by a bright light—the light of Christ. That summer night was one of the most powerful experiences of my life. After this experience, when I thought of Mom, I could smile, tell stories about her, and remember the good times instead of the nightmare of her death. That's when I knew healing had taken place. It was a big lesson on the healing power of God.

God gave me that gift in order to help other people heal their wounds. The method of going back to the wound and asking the Lord to be present was powerful. Jesus promised that he would be with us until the end of the age. He's always loving us. It was huge for my healing, my spiritual life, and then in my life as a priest. As God has brought me through the most difficult experience of my life, I know that I can face anything with him. What I had feared most in life was never my own death, but my mother's. She and I were so close that I thought there was no way I could live without her. It took two years, but I finally realized that with God I could get through anything. I had confidence that no matter what situation I faced, God would help me through it. With the healing came a new confidence. I had to remain grounded in my faith in God. He can bring good things out of the worst circumstances. It didn't mean that I wanted to live through anything like that again, but I knew that with God, I could.

That summer I learned that I truly am a beloved child of God, like everyone else. He showed me that his love is unconditional and beyond my wildest imagination. I also learned that I need people I can trust in order to let my guard down and be myself. My friends have helped me through difficult times by listening and not judging.

God is the greatest friend of all. He wants us to come to him with everything—the good, the bad, and the ugly. He not only wants us to survive these experiences; he wants us to thrive in them with his help and grace.

CHAPTER SIX

FATHER WHAT-A-WASTE!

I have had two experiences that would mark my life forever: Mom's death on July 7, 1998, and that night in chapel in the summer of 2000. Through the most difficult times in life, we grow the most. The key is letting God in to heal and not trying to do it alone. I tried to deal with my grief myself, but I developed an unhealthy self-reliance instead of a strong reliance on God. I became angry and couldn't see an end to my suffering. I thank God for my friend Dennis and for a great spiritual director that summer in Omaha. Without them, I don't think I would have found healing for many years.

I was confident that God was calling me to be a priest. I had two more years of seminary left, and I rested in the profound peace that I was where I was supposed to be and doing what I was supposed to be doing. God kept showing me that this was his will for me. I had seen the cardinal in the tree after Mom's death when I had cried out for a sign. Her friends had told me at her wake that Mom always thought I was going to be a priest. Sometime later, I also had a dream about Mom. The details of the dream have not remained with me over the years. But I can remember my mother saying something like this to me: "Heaven is real, Jesus is real, and don't stop doing what you're doing." All of these were significant affirmations of my vocation. More than any of the signs, I just knew. Everything within me urged me forward. With the grace of God, I prayed that I would be ready for the challenges that would come.

Through the death of my mother, I learned that life is not about material things but about relationships with God and others: loving the Lord with all my heart, mind, and soul, and loving my neighbor as myself. This lesson was reaffirmed by my time in the seminary. The men who studied around me became my brothers. We grew closer to Christ, to one another, and to our call to the priesthood. It was a brotherhood that could not be easily broken, and it was even deeper than the brotherhood I experienced playing baseball.

We arrived at Mundelein from varying backgrounds. The seminary could take converts like me, who hardly knew anything about the Bible or theology, and, through the power of the Holy Spirit, help them become priests after the heart of Christ. I didn't know Scripture at all when I started, but now I have a passion for it. One of my favorite things to do is to read the Bible and apply it to everyday life, which is something I began doing early on in seminary.

Some friends back home were going through difficult times. I started sending them the Mass readings from the day with a few lines of encouragement. They enjoyed the messages and spread the word about them widely. In a few months, I was emailing messages to more than a thousand people. To serve them better, I created a blog that made it much easier for me to communicate with my readers. This online ministry really took off, and I continued it after I was ordained. More than thirteen thousand people have subscribed to it, and the list is still growing.[*]

When people tell me that I have a gift for writing, I tell them that all that I am and all that I have is a gift from God and there is no reason for me to boast. People sometimes say that they don't

---

[*] You can subscribe to Fr. Burke's blog at www.frburke23.wordpress.com.

think God has gifted them in any way. I gently correct them, explaining that God has gifted each one of us in special ways.

* * *

I spent five years in the seminary, from the fall of 1997 until the spring of 2002. The seminary faculty measured our growth in four areas of formation: human, spiritual, intellectual, and pastoral. Our human development was the foundation of everything, as grace builds upon nature. We were encouraged to have a healthy balance of diet, exercise, sleep, leisure, and friendship. Our spiritual formation included Mass, personal and communal prayer, spiritual direction, and spiritual reading. Classes and seminars in philosophy and theology formed us intellectually. We studied morality, Scripture, Church history, canon law, and many other subjects. Pastoral formation gave us hands-on experience, like visiting a nursing home, serving as a hospital chaplain, and interning in a parish. The training we received helped us become more like Jesus every day. Then when we became priests, we would represent Christ to his people.

To supplement our seminary formation, the diocese gave us different summer assignments. In the summer of 1998, the diocese allowed me to stay with my mom during her illness and then with my dad after her death. I spent the next summer in Cuernavaca, Mexico, learning Spanish. I had been away from the language for fourteen years, but I had a strong foundation—four years in high school and one semester in college. I was excited about becoming more proficient because Joliet had a large Spanish-speaking population. In Cuernavaca, I lived with an older couple across the street from our Spanish school.

I fell in love with Mexico that summer. I loved learning the culture and traditions of the Mexican people, and I admired how they integrated their strong faith into their everyday lives. Learning a new culture expanded my horizons. (I thought acquiring another language would enable me to evangelize more people. I never imagined the bishop would one day assign me to a bilingual parish. How wrong I was.)

Internships were another wonderful part of Mundelein's formation program. From February to May 2000, I interned at St. Philip the Apostle Parish in Addison, Illinois. I lived in the parish and shadowed Fr. Tom Sularz, who was an amazing mentor. I saw how much Fr. Tom loved the people and valued his priestly ministry. He took me with him to visit people in the hospital and those who were homebound. I observed him as he celebrated Mass and preached. I saw how the people responded to him, and I knew how blessed I was to have him as my mentor. He was a great example for what it means to serve as a priest. Fr. Tom passed away in 2018. God rest his soul.

The internship is often a make-or-break experience for seminarians. We get a taste of what our future will be like. The seminary has a difficult time simulating parish life, but the internship is the closest we can get without being ordained. It helps us discern if the priesthood is truly our vocation. I found myself coming alive in the parish environment. This experience sealed it for me.

One of my favorite things to do, and still is, was joining families for dinner in their homes, where they felt comfortable sharing about their lives and faith journeys. A good shepherd knows his sheep, and this was a fun way to get to know the flock. I knew in my heart that God was calling me to be a diocesan priest, one who lives in a parish and has regular contact with families. I couldn't wait to bring the sacraments of the Eucharist and Reconciliation to his people and walk with them on their journey of faith.

After the internship, I spent the summer of 2000 in Omaha, Nebraska, with my brother seminarians Dennis and John at the Institute for Priestly Formation. There I found the powerful healing that I shared above. With the help of the Holy Spirit, they had us name our core wounds and gave us tools to help us receive healing. Another great takeaway from the IPF was learning about the five identities of a diocesan priest: beloved son, chaste spouse, spiritual father, spiritual physician, and head and shepherd. They helped me understand how to grow in my fundamental identity as a beloved son of God the Father. All the other identities derive their meaning from knowing my relationship with the Father. Identifying as a child of God is true not only for priests but for all people. When we come to know this truth in the depths of our hearts, everything changes.

* * *

During the summer of 2001, my final internship before ordination, I was assigned to a clinical pastoral experience (CPE) at Good Samaritan Hospital in Downers Grove, Illinois. CPE trains seminarians to serve as chaplains and to take care of the pastoral needs of patients from all faiths. Working in the emergency room was my biggest fear about CPE. I never was good with blood. I prayed that I would be assigned anywhere but there. And, of course, my first day at the hospital I was assigned to the ER. God knew that I had to face my fears to overcome them.

I cared for family members after the doctors told them that their loved ones had just passed away. I remember a wife who wanted to see her husband's body after he had been nearly decapitated in a motorcycle accident. I tried to talk her out of seeing him, but she wanted to say goodbye. I worked with the nurses to situate his body so that he looked as presentable as possible. Her cries of grief brought me to tears. I could say nothing to make things better, but I believe my presence gave her some comfort amid this extreme shock. She didn't want to leave, but after about ten minutes, she said her goodbyes and I walked her out to a private family room. I learned the importance of the ministry of presence in the hospital.

There were many graces in difficult situations. I watched in awe as the doctors and nurses sprang into action and responded to each patient with precision and care. I saw the love and concern of medical professionals for their patients. Even though I still do not enjoy emergencies, I feel comfortable going into most situations that involve illness, death, and dying. I learned that it was not me, Burke, who was ministering to these people; it was Jesus Christ who was working through me. When I learned that I needed to decrease so that the Lord could increase in me, I felt no pressure to have the right words to say. Many times, the situation called for no words. The ministry of presence was all that some people needed.

* * *

A few nurses in the ER called me "Father What-a-Waste" when I walked in. I just laughed it off, but it did spark questions from them about why priests don't get married. This allowed for some good conversations about celibacy. It also helped me to work through my own feelings about it and share them with others. Our culture is so oversexualized, and people think that if you are not having relations, you can't be happy. I explained to the nurses that some people have sex but no intimacy. And some people who don't have sexual relations have a lot of intimacy. The world equates intimacy with sex, but real intimacy is meeting another person at the deepest level of the heart. People open their hearts to priests all the time through confession, counseling, or casual meetings. In these conversations with people, priests can enjoy intimacy every day, and it is fulfilling.

Some people think that the Church should change its teaching on celibacy, but I believe that the world needs celibacy. Our unmarried, chaste lives on earth point people to what life will be like in heaven. I have had many passionate conversations with people who say that celibacy is not normal. They are right in the sense that most people are not called to live celibate lives. But for those of us who are called to live as celibates, it is a great gift.

God willing, when we get to heaven, we will experience God's love and intimacy in a powerful way. I trust that the Lord will fulfill our deepest desires.

* * *

On Friday, October 26, 2001, my friend Bishop Robert Kaffer ordained me as transitional deacon at the St. Charles Borromeo Pastoral Center in Romeoville, Illinois. The word "transitional" means that I was on my way to becoming a priest. (Permanent deacons are ordained clergy and are not moving toward the priesthood.) We make a promise of celibacy at the diaconate ordination, which is a big deal. Taking the vow was not a difficult thing for me after the prayer and preparation of the previous five years. At the time I did not understand everything that it meant, much like a newly married couple who have no idea what's in store for them. No one knows the joys and struggles that will come. But I trust in God.

Hearing God's call and following it has been one of my greatest lessons. Before I went to seminary, I thought that celibacy would lead to a lonely, poor, and boring life. I wondered why God would call me to something that would make me miserable. By following the Lord's will, I have discovered that this life is more rewarding than I could imagine. We cannot outdo God in generosity. I have met wonderful people, who have shared intimate details of their lives with me. Prudently, of course, I share myself with them as well. These relationships are the source of fulfillment not only in the priesthood but also in life in general.

A beautiful moment in the ordination Mass occurs when the candidates lie prostrate on the floor, nose to the ground. This symbolizes that we are laying down our lives for the Lord and becoming a bridge between the people and God. After we made the promise of celibacy and promised to pray the Liturgy of the

Hours for the Church and her people, the bishop laid hands on us. He called down the Holy Spirit upon us so that our lives would be ordered to Christ. It was a joyful evening. My whole family attended the Mass and celebrated with me afterward, although most of them were not Catholic.

I was assigned as a deacon to the Cathedral of St. Raymond Nonnatus. I had six months left in the seminary, but on weekends I drove the seventy-five minutes to the cathedral to preach, baptize, and perform other ministries. I was excited to minister as an ordained deacon. People opened their hearts and homes to me very quickly. I loved getting hands-on experience at the cathedral.

Most exciting for me was the opportunity to preach homilies. I enjoyed the preparation for preaching: praying with Scripture, reading the Church Fathers, and listening to the homilies of Father (now Bishop) Robert Barron. I experimented with preaching in front of the altar and at the ambo. I didn't read my homilies but spoke from the heart after much preparation, study, and prayer.

I don't remember what I preached about in my very first homily, but I know I was humbled to preach the Word of God. Although I was very nervous, I felt the power of the Holy Spirit giving me strength and the words to speak. It was much like playing baseball. I would prepare diligently by watching film, practicing, and studying the opponents' tendencies. Before each game, I would get butterflies in my stomach. Once I got my first at bat or fielded the first ground ball, the nerves were gone, and I could focus on investing myself in the game. My experience has been the same every time I preach. I get butterflies because I realize this is a great responsibility to preach the Word of God for his people. Once I start speaking, the nerves subside, and I can allow the Holy Spirit to guide me in the homily. I was especially nervous in that first homily as a deacon, so it took a while longer for the nerves to calm.

* * *

Although I loved this time as a deacon, I anticipated my priestly ordination as it approached on June 1, 2002.

This was the day my life changed forever. It was the day I promised obedience to my bishop and his successors. It was the day I promised to orient my life to Christ in a radical way. It was the day I was ordained a priest next to four other men, including my friend Dennis. I was more excited and joyful than I was rounding the bases for my grand slam. My ordination was my second grand slam in the playing field of the Lord.

Dad, Jan, my brothers, and my brothers' families were right behind me in the front pew on the left side of the church. They witnessed this ancient rite of ordination of priests. Later, they said that you could not wipe the smile off my face that day. I remember being full of joy—immense and indescribable joy. "I'm doing what God created me to do," I kept thinking. Couples who get married say that although they were nervous, they knew that they were meant to spend their lives with each other. They knew that marriage was their vocation. That was my experience as well. I knew that this was what I was supposed to do.

My brother Brock had a powerful experience at the ordination Mass. His wife, Maggie, had been encouraging him to join her and their three children in the Catholic Church. She was raised Catholic and has a beautiful faith. She brought the kids to Sunday Mass and was raising them in the Church. My brother had not always been on the same page spiritually. My prostration during the ordination Mass—as I laid down my life for Christ—surprised all my family, especially Brock. They were close to the action, and they were all crying. Brock decided that if his little brother was willing to lay down his life for Christ, he was going to join him. He began to attend the RCIA back in Colorado shortly after my ordination and joined the Church the next Easter.

After our ordination Mass, Dennis and I had a combined reception at Ingalls Park. Our families had made posters with hundreds of pictures of us and put them all around the hall. I was full of joy and peace that day. It felt like all was right with the world. When we find our vocational call and follow it, a peace that goes beyond all understanding envelops us.

The next morning, I celebrated my Mass of Thanksgiving at the cathedral. It was nerve racking. I had asked my good friend Deacon Ed Petak to serve the Mass with me. He would be there to guide me, and his presence calmed me. I had attended thousands of Masses, but it took on a whole new meaning when I was the one presiding. I was worried about missing parts or messing up, but I calmed down when it came time for the homily. I have always enjoyed preaching. As a deacon, as a young priest, and today, it is still one of my favorite things to do. I love to share the Word of God and make it relevant. I want to give people something they can take home and put into practice.

One of my most prized possessions is the chalice that Dad and Jan bought me for ordination, which I used for my first Mass. After Mom had passed, Dad gave me her wedding ring. He explained that since he had two daughters-in-law, he couldn't choose between them. And he thought that Mom would want me to have the ring. When Dad and Jan gave me the chalice, I knew that I wanted to put Mom's ring on it. We had the ring soldered onto its stem, so every time I use it at Mass, I see it, touch it, and remember to pray for my dear mother.

* * *

I was ordained on June 1, 2002, right after the priest abuse scandal broke in Boston. It had touched our diocese, and there were protesters outside the cathedral the morning of our ordination. Appalled, Dad asked me bluntly, "Are you sure you want to be a part of this?"

"Dad," I answered without hesitation, "I want to be a part of the solution."

Many seminarians and young priests repeat the same words to family and friends when they are confronted with the same question. The scandal has been horrible, especially seeing that many priests had taken advantage of their position to abuse innocent children. It never should have happened even one time.

God can bring good out of every bad situation. Since the scandal broke, the motives for men to enter seminary have been purified. Before the scandal, priests were put on a pedestal without having to earn people's trust. In the past, Catholics and many non-Catholics revered all priests. I think this esteem invited some men to seek the priesthood without having a vocation, because they wanted to be looked up to by other people. Today, young men know that they are not going to be put on a pedestal. In fact, people who don't know us might look at us and think, "Are you one of those bad priests?"

I believe that this unworthy motive for men entering the seminary is gone. Men who present themselves now are more likely to have a true call from God. Priests must earn people's respect just like everyone else, and that's a healthy result of the scandal. Hopefully we can continue to bring justice to the victims and earn the trust of people once again. The goal of the devil is to separate, isolate, and conquer. He wants people to leave the Church because it's a wonderful vessel that helps so many people get to heaven. I encourage us all to stick together and allow the love and mercy of Christ to show forth from the Church.

* * *

About a month prior to our ordination, the bishop gave us our first parish assignments. A week before the bishop contacted me, a priest from the diocese called me.

"Hey Burke," he said, "I heard you're going to St. Isaac Jogues in Hinsdale."

He seemed to be a well-connected guy; I believed him and spent the next week researching the parish in Hinsdale. St. Isaac Jogues is one of the wealthiest parishes in the diocese with a beautiful church and a predominantly English-speaking population. I was excited about the prospect of going there.

A week later, Bishop Imesch called me at the seminary.

"Burke! I've got good news!" he said. "You're going to St. Mary's in West Chicago."

I was glad this conversation took place over the phone because my jaw probably hit the floor. I knew little about West Chicago, but I did know it was a Spanish-speaking parish. I think the bishop had heard that I was proficient in Spanish, which I wasn't. I could read Spanish well, but I wasn't fluent. I knew I was not ready to minister in Spanish. What was I going to do? I thought about making a request to change parishes. Maybe I could only serve at the English Masses? Maybe I could get through a year and then transfer? I did not want to be the guy who immediately asked for a change. I still struggled a little with perfectionism, and I wanted to rise to the challenge, but this was going to be one challenge too big for me to face alone.

CHAPTER SEVEN

A FRIEND OF JESÚS

In the Joliet diocese, the third Wednesday of June was the day when all the newly ordained priests began their assignments, as did anyone changing assignments. And June 19, 2002, was my first day at St. Mary's in West Chicago. I was excited to start my priestly ministry and the next chapter of my life. I was incredibly nervous about ministering in Spanish. I did not want to let the bishop or pastor down, but I knew that my Spanish was not at the level they expected.

Dad and Jan helped me move my clothes, books, and small necessities into the rectory. There was a new bed awaiting me, along with bedroom and office furniture. I arrived the same day as St. Mary's pastor, Fr. Bill Conway. He'd been there twice before—as a seminarian and then as the associate pastor. He was now the pastor, and we were starting together on the same day. He gave me a warm welcome and saw to it that I had everything I needed.

St. Mary's was an entirely new world. West Chicago is about 80 percent Spanish-speaking. Not only was I learning how to be a priest, but I had to do it in two languages, with most of it being in my second language. Seminary prepared us well for priesthood, but like many vocations, you have to learn a lot on the go. The first couple of days were overwhelming; I felt like I was going to fail.

Perfectionism reared its ugly head again. I could not be perfect without being fluent and confident in Spanish.

My first Saturday there, only three days after I arrived, Fr. Bill and I walked over to the church to hear confessions before the vigil Mass.

"Okay, Bill," I said, "you'll hear the Spanish confessions, and I'll hear the English ones."

"Nope," he replied. "We're not going to put up signs. People can go to either one of us."

I did not realize that almost all the confessions would be in Spanish. If we had twenty confessions on any given day, an average of nineteen would be in Spanish. And the first ten I heard were Spanish speakers. I couldn't understand them because they talked so fast. I gave them all one Ave Maria for their penance. They went away pretty happy. As weeks passed, my confession line got longer as the news spread: "El Padrecito no entiende el Español (Father doesn't understand Spanish). You can tell him anything, and he'll give you one Ave Maria as a penance."

From my first weekend in West Chicago, I celebrated Mass in Spanish. I read the Scriptures and the prayers very well, but the preaching was hard. I had to write my homily down and read it during Mass. I couldn't speak off the cuff, which meant I stood in the pulpit, glancing up at the people occasionally as I read it. I could see people's eyes closing as they fell asleep. I was boring them to death. I was dripping with sweat because there was no air conditioning, and I was extremely nervous. My hands were shaking and my knees knocking. I knew this whole assignment was going to be difficult, and it was only the beginning. What was I going to do?

It hit me that this was going to be the biggest challenge of my life. My time as a priest had begun with so much hope, and now I faced four years of putting people to sleep in the pews. I felt like I was less than half a priest because I could only communicate with about twenty percent of the parishioners. I called Dad after that first weekend. I didn't realize how down I sounded. As soon as he got off the phone, he told Jan, "Something is really wrong with Burke." Within an hour they were at the rectory, asking me how I was doing. I was thankful for their visit. They lifted my spirits and encouraged me to do my best, which was all I could do. It was exactly what I needed to hear.

One morning during my second week at St. Mary's, I went to the church to celebrate Mass. (Thankfully, all but one of our weekday Masses were in English.) As I walked to the beautiful old church, I was going over my homily in my head. Apparently, I was not the only person preaching that morning. A huge man stood in front of the altar declaring, "I'm Jesus Christ. Repent from your sins!" I thought, "They didn't prepare me for this in seminary."

The people looked at me with fear in their eyes as if to say, "What are you going to do?" Well, I didn't know what to do. I needed time to think and pray. Like a scared little kid, I walked right to the sacristy to get vested for Mass, begging God for a solution to this problem. I had to walk past the guy to get there. This giant could probably kill me with one punch; he was so huge. I had just begun praying in the sacristy when it got quiet in the church. I peeked out and saw that the man had seated himself in the third pew. "Okay, good," I thought, and I went out for the Mass.

Everything went smoothly until the homily. Periodically, the man would shout loud remarks as I preached. Each time, everyone jumped, including me, but we made it through Mass with no major difficulties. At the end of Mass, Jan, our parish nurse, told me that she knew the man. She said that he had Tourette syndrome and that he had escaped from a local mental health facility. She called them, and they promised to send someone to pick him up. I remember the care Jan showed for this man. They sat side by side on the church stairs, having a conversation. She was teaching me how to handle situations in a crisis with a gentleness different than some of the harder approaches I had experienced in the hospital.

The way everyone had looked at me before Mass stayed with me. They seemed to say, "Father, this is your responsibility." I was in a leadership role that went beyond helping people in their spiritual lives. They expected me to step up in these situations. They were looking for a spiritual father and leader.

Besides my struggle with the language, my assignment to St. Mary's presented a difficult situation in the rectory. When you marry someone, you choose that person. You are probably around the same age and have similar likes and dislikes. But a priest often gets put into a rectory with someone from a different generation. And your interests, your ecclesiology, and your ideology may differ a lot.

That's what happened to me. Fr. Bill was a good pastor, but I had to learn how to live with his interests and preferences that were not like mine. We had a big age gap. He was fifty-five years old, and I was thirty-five. He was into the arts more than sports; I loved sports but was not a big fan of the arts. We were almost complete opposites. Fr. Bill had received his training from a religious order, and he led the rectory like a community with common meals, common prayer, and a regular schedule. I wanted to spend time with him, but the seminary had formed me to take time to be out and about with the people. We recognized that our formation and desires were different and that we would have to talk things through. Over time, we came to an agreement that it was important to pray and eat together, but not all the time.

Fr. Bill knew a great deal about Mexican history and culture, and he taught me how to minister to the Hispanic community. He also showed me the importance of presenting a united front to the parishioners, even when we had problems in the rectory. How could we preach about love, unity, and family if the people never saw us together or thought we were not getting along? Actions speak louder than words. We didn't fight a lot, but we did have some arguments. I appreciated that we greeted people after all the Masses together. We showed them our unity, even if we were not on the same page all the time in the rectory. This is much like family life. My parents taught us not to air our dirty laundry in public. If we were having problems in the house, we did not need to publicize that to the world.

* * *

Every time I felt like I was getting my footing, the language barrier would sneak up and knock me down again. A couple times, I got close to calling the bishop to tell him that I could not do this and to ask him to send me to an English-speaking parish. I was ready to call it quits on ministering in Spanish. I had tried for months, and it wasn't getting any better or any easier.

It was about that time that Jesús Fernandez, a parishioner at St. Mary's, called me up and said, "Hey, I see you're struggling. Why don't we go out for dinner?" At dinner, he told me that he would help me. "Bring your homilies over each week. I will read them and work with you." I was struck by this man's kindness. He not only wanted to help me as his priest; he wanted to be my friend.

For the first time, I thought that staying at St. Mary's might work out. Jesús and his family went out of their way to help me. Starting that week, I wrote my homily out in English and Spanish, and then I brought it to Jesús for his corrections. He took out his red pen and edited it. Some phrases I used were textbook perfect, but Jesús explained to me that this was not what the people would understand. Practically speaking, I had to learn a whole new language. The key was communicating the Gospel, not being textbook perfect. Jesús jokingly gave me an "F" for my Spanish on that first homily, but he was very encouraging. I took my marked-up homily back to the rectory, feeling hopeful for the first time. I changed it according to Jesús' recommendations. The tedious review process took hours out of both our schedules every week, but it was so helpful. Slowly, I began to learn, and a lifelong friendship was emerging.

One night we had a Reconciliation service with about five other priests. St. Mary's was a small church, holding only about 250 people. There were no confessionals. I was up in the choir loft hearing confessions. The Spanish confessions had become easier the more I heard them. It was still difficult to understand some of the Spanish speakers, but it didn't seem like they were speaking so fast anymore. My ear was becoming accustomed to the language, like it had when I was studying in Mexico.

All the confessions that night were face-to-face, with the two chairs slightly apart. One Hispanic man in his thirties knelt instead of sitting and put his elbows on my knees. It made me very uncomfortable. What about boundaries? What about my personal space? But, as his confession continued, I realized that he trusted me so much that he wanted to make physical contact with me. This man, only a few years younger than me, spoke like he was talking to his dad. It was such a tender, fatherly moment. I was learning that personal space was much smaller in the Hispanic community. They wanted to be close, especially to their priest, their father. I started to enjoy the closeness while also maintaining healthy boundaries. They wanted their priest to be a part of their everyday lives.

After Mass people would grab my hand and kiss it. The first time it happened, I drew back my hand. I didn't want anyone to venerate me. I thought they were putting me on a pedestal, and I didn't want that. The Filipinos in the community took my hand and touched their forehead as a sign of blessing. In both cases, I was uncomfortable.

"I don't deserve that," I told Jesús, referring to people kissing my hand. "I am a sinner just like them. It's really uncomfortable for me. Why do they do that?"

"It's not about you at all," Jesús said. "It's about the priesthood. What they are doing is honoring the consecrated hands of a priest. Your hands bring them Jesus in the Eucharist."

When I understood that it wasn't about me but about the priesthood, I accepted it. I was okay with anyone honoring Jesus and recognizing that I am his servant.

The Hispanic community also loved to hug and kiss one another on the cheek. The Masters family had never been very big on hugging or kissing. But living in West Chicago helped me to become more comfortable with these signs of affection than I ever thought I'd be. Now it's a part of me. When I'm in the Anglo culture, I have to remind myself to hold back a bit. I appreciate the family atmosphere that I sense in the Hispanic culture. Another thing I appreciated in the community was the way they greeted one another when entering and leaving a room. I was raised to simply say hello and goodbye in a general way to everyone at the same time. In the Hispanic culture, they come around and greet everyone upon arriving and leaving. I warmed up to this custom very easily.

Another big cultural surprise occurred when I went to do my first house blessing. I didn't know how important this event was in the Latino culture. I just thought I'd go, pray the rite of blessing of a new home, sprinkle some holy water, chat with the family, and be on my way quickly. The first time I was invited to do house blessings, I scheduled three of them consecutively at 10 a.m., 11 a.m., and 12 p.m. I took Jesús with me to help me with small talk in Spanish. He went with me to house blessings as well as nursing homes and hospitals. He could help me with translations if I needed it. He loved the ministry and became a dear companion of mine through all the time we spent together.

When we arrived at the first house, there were about fifty people outside. All the extended family had been invited, and they had a huge cookout. I had expected it to be just the homeowners in a quiet, low-key affair. I asked Jesús if this was how it always was, and he said yes. He told me that if you don't eat their food, they get offended. It was a big deal, and I learned from then on that I would never schedule multiple house blessings in one day. It was wonderful, though, that something I had thought of as simple was a big family event. Not having grown up Catholic, I had never thought about having my house blessed. I never knew the beauty of a house blessing or how important blessings, sacraments, and sacramentals can be in a culture.

* * *

After about a year of editing and rewriting my homilies, Jesús took my notes away. "You don't need them anymore," he said.

"What are you doing?" I asked. "I need those notes!"

He refused. "Your Spanish is good enough," he told me encouragingly. "Why don't you come out away from the ambo and just speak to us? Speak from your heart. You can do it."

I trusted both Jesús and Jesus. I trusted that Jesús knew what he was doing, but I did not trust my Spanish. He said, "If you get stuck, just ask, 'Como se dice . . .' and then say in English the word that has you stumped." Many of the people were bilingual, and he assured me that they'd help me out.

The next Sunday, after reading the Gospel, I stood in front of the altar and started talking. I stumbled over many words, but like Jesús said, people kindly offered the words I was looking for in Spanish. They paid more attention because they were assisting me with the language. They had to follow the homily so that they had the correct context to help me. Jesús knew what he was doing. The homily now served a dual purpose: people paid more attention, and I became more confident in Spanish.

Even though my Spanish was poor, I received support from the Hispanic community. "Keep going Father! You're getting better," they would say after Mass. That encouragement spurred me to keep working diligently. Thanks be to God, after four years at St. Mary's, I not only felt confident speaking Spanish but also had a deep desire to do more bilingual ministry.

* * *

God continually showed me during my time at St. Mary's that he doesn't differentiate by skin color, language, ethnicity, or country of origin. He has adopted all of us, which makes all of us brothers and sisters in Christ. As our country continues to go through difficult times with race relations, I believe the answer is for each of us to find our identity as beloved brothers and sisters in Christ, because we are all children of God. And we are all looking for the same thing: we want to love and be loved. The more we realize how much God loves us, the more we are able to love our neighbor.

I remember an eighth grader once asking me, "Father, do you see the world differently as a priest?" I was stunned by his mature question, and after a moment of thought, I responded, "I see everyone as part of my family." This shouldn't be true only for priests. We should see every person as part of the same human family, a brother or sister in Christ and a fellow beloved child of God the Father.

After I could speak Spanish fluently, I enjoyed being in the parish more. But it was like having two separate parishes: the English-speaking community and the Spanish-speaking community. We held parties together as one community, which were great. Ultimately, though, the culture and the language created a divide. Luckily, there were some people, like Jesús, who were bilingual and bicultural and could bridge the gap between the two communities.

I especially loved the Hispanic community's desire to involve their priest in their family life. If a teenager had trouble in school, instead of taking them right to a psychologist or school counselor, their parents brought them first to talk to Father. The concept was foreign to me, but it amazed me that I became a father figure for these families. It was so powerful for me to take on the identity of a spiritual father for so many people.

The first day at the parish, I walked into the sacristy, and the sacristan, who was seventy-five years old, greeted me, saying, "Good morning, Father!" I was a young, thirty-five-year-old, newly ordained priest, and this man called me "Father." It hit me that this was who I was. I was not just Burke anymore. I was now called to be a spiritual father to all these people. Gradually, I grew accustomed to being called "Father" and to the responsibilities of the priesthood. As my earthly father worked multiple jobs to take care of his family, it was my responsibility to work hard to take care of my spiritual family in the parish. Just as I had learned to grow into my identity as a beloved son, the Lord was teaching me what it meant to be a spiritual father.

CHAPTER EIGHT

LIVING IN THE MOMENT

In the parish, I organized my office how I liked it. I was, and still am, a list maker. I maintain a list of the things I need to do. I feel a sense of accomplishment when I cross something off the list. But during my first year at St. Mary's, it seemed when I tried to do something on the list, our receptionist called me, saying, "Fr. Burke, can you see this person?" I always said yes. I met with the person and got back to my list, only to hear, "Father, can you go to the hospital to anoint a parishioner?"

Few people called to make an appointment. This clashed with my perfectionist desire to schedule everything, complete my to-do list, and leave my office with a clean desk every day. Messy parish life wasn't how I was used to operating. I got frustrated because nothing was getting checked off my list. Instead, my list was getting longer every day. And some things never seemed to get finished, which made me uptight. I had to realize I will never be caught up and, as a priest, switch gears. This was a hard shift for me, but it happened by the grace of God.

I took my frustration to my spiritual director. He helped me realize that the interruptions to my schedule were the most powerful moments that I had every day. God showed me that he was in the interruptions. I sensed that God was saying to me, "You may have your day planned out, but I want you to live according to *my* plan. Live in the moment. Make a list, but be flexible." In response, I prayed for the grace to live in the moment, and I began to welcome the interruptions as opportunities to encounter the Lord in every person that I met.

Bishop J. Peter Sartain was a great example for me of someone who was able to live in the moment. I started as vocation director the same week that he became our new bishop in 2006. Our cathedral was packed for his installation, and after Mass a line of people waiting to greet him wrapped around the whole cathedral. As I watched him taking time with each person, I got concerned about how long people at the end of the line would have to wait. The more I watched the bishop greet people, the more I realized that he was with every person for as long as they needed. He was present to each person. I talked to some people after they met with him, and they said that it felt like they were the only person in the room when they were speaking to him. It reminded me of my mother, who had this gift as well.

When I read the lives of the saints—which I love to do—I notice that they all seem to have the ability to live in the moment and to love the person right in front of them. Mother Teresa and John Paul II are great examples. I have spoken to many people who have met these two modern-day saints. Everyone tells me the same thing: they felt like Mother Teresa or John Paul II was present to them, and to them alone. Watching Bishop Sartain that day, I decided that I wanted to live in the moment and to show the same kindness to the people around me. I had always lived in the future, thinking: What's next? What about after that? Then what? That kind of thinking would take me right out of the present moment. I'd be with a person, but I'd be thinking about the things on my list I needed to do later. I wouldn't be fully present to the person right in front of me.

In West Chicago, I had started learning to love the person in each interruption. Then Bishop Sartain showed me what holiness looks like as he gave his laser focus to each person in the receiving line. God was teaching me not be a slave to my list. I wanted to live according to God's plan, not mine. Our culture teaches us to "just do it," to "follow your dreams," to "get what you want out of life." But I have learned that the key to holiness and happiness is to follow the Holy Spirit's prompting in the present moment.

* * *

Although I had opened my heart more to God's plan, I was nervous when Fr. Bill put me in charge of the youth group. Sure, I was closer in age to the kids than he was, but I had never worked with teens. I was more at ease with people my age and older, probably because as the baby of the family I was constantly surrounded by older people. I was not about to back down from this challenge though. I love a good challenge!

I used my sports background, hoping it would be the best way to connect with the kids. I gathered some young adults to help me, and they were a great support. Not everyone loves sports, so we found other things, like art and music, as ways of connecting with the teens. We'd play baseball, football, or soccer, and then we'd have a talk that centered on a message from Scripture or a Church teaching. The kids responded with enthusiasm, and I enjoyed working with them. I learned that God does not take away what we love when we decide to follow him. He didn't waste my love for baseball; he used it to help me relate to others in ministry.

My first choice would've been to work with adults, but God brought me to youth. We serve a God of surprises, and I have learned to expect the unexpected with the Lord. In his perfect way, he was preparing me to become a vocation director to help young people discern their calling. I would not have been ready for that role had Fr. Bill not asked me to be the youth minister at St. Mary's parish. God seems to send me where I need to be stretched, like when I was placed in the emergency room as a hospital chaplain. I have come to welcome change, challenges, and surprises because we serve a God who has amazing plans for us.

With my high school ministry team, I started a Kairos retreat for the parish. Most of our kids at St. Mary's went to public school. I wanted to give them an opportunity to go on a retreat and encounter Christ as I had in high school. Since this would be our first Kairos at St. Mary's, we invited St. Mary's parish in DeKalb to lead the retreat. They had been holding Kairos retreats for a few years.

The St. Mary's Kairos was an amazing experience for our kids. The Kairos helped them know themselves better and know the love of God personally. One of the talks, called "Life Graph," was given by an adult. He described the different highs and lows of his life and let the teens reflect on their lives as well. Teen peers gave talks sharing how they came to know Jesus in their own way. And they shared with us how they met the person of Jesus in the sacraments, especially in the Eucharist and Reconciliation. The kids had opportunities to share their experiences with one another and later with their parents.

My Kairos had a big impact on my life because it was there that I first started the journey of believing that I was a beloved son of God. My prayer is that our young teens will also come to know their identity as children of God and that God loves them unconditionally. They hear so many voices that make them doubt the reality of God. Kairos was one of the game-changers in my life. That is why I have tried to bring Kairos not only to our Catholic school students but also the public high school students.

During that first Kairos retreat with St. Mary's of DeKalb, one of our girls connected with one of their boys. They were drawn to each other. I wasn't happy about their flirting. But they ended up dating and getting married years later. All that we do can have a profound impact on someone else's life. Now they are soulmates and have four wonderful sons. I often think about the fact that had we not held this retreat, maybe Mary and Tom would have never met. Everything matters, even things that seem relatively small. I had discouraged the boys and girls from pairing off at Kairos, but God had other plans for those two.

* * *

When I became a priest, I had a hard time saying no to anything. Our rector in the seminary told us repeatedly, "Always say yes." He was telling us that life's not about us; it's about serving the Lord and laying down our lives in a radical way for others. But I have learned that if I say yes to every good thing, I may not be doing the best thing with my time. We can spread ourselves so thin that we may suffer physically, spiritually, and emotionally, and we may not be able to do what God created us to do. This was an important lesson for me: I often have to say no to the good so that I can say yes to the great things God has in store.

The seminary encouraged us to wait a few years before we started doing spiritual direction. I knew I would serve others better if I was well established in my priesthood. But, probably out of pride, I started giving young adults direction and counseling right away. They were happy to have a young priest to care for them, and spiritual direction was going really well at first. But in the same week, I had two young women tell me that they had fallen in love with me. Both women were struggling in their marriages. I told them that I could no longer be their spiritual director and that I would help them find another one. It was an awkward situation; they were parishioners that I would see at Mass and around the parish.

It is a good and holy desire to help everyone, but we must recognize our limitations and refer people to someone else, like an older priest, a professional therapist, or a well-respected married couple. After my experience with the two women from the parish, I saw the importance of befriending couples in solid marriages.

Two people in a holy marriage inspire me to be faithful to my vocation and my call to holiness. And married couples have told me that my faithfulness to my vocation inspires them in theirs.

* * *

As a young priest, I wondered if I would ever see a miracle. In the seminary, they warned us about having a messiah complex. Sometimes priests get ordained and think they are the messiah and with the help of God can save the whole world. Instead, we should just focus on doing our part in the greater mission of Christ in the Church. Despite the warning, I thought I could save the world. So, during the first year of my priesthood, I expected to see miraculous things happening all around me. I was not content seeing God in the everyday situations of life. Thus, I was disappointed and a little disillusioned because I was not seeing miracles. I sometimes even doubted that Jesus was active in the sacraments and in the world. But as I was to learn, God always meets us where we are.

One day I got a call to go to the hospital to anoint Irasema, a twelve-year-old girl from West Chicago. The hospital told her parents that she had only a few weeks to live. Her body was being ravaged by a rare disease. I asked my friend Jesús to come with me to the hospital because the family only spoke Spanish. They were completely devastated, as you can imagine. I remember my fear walking into this situation because it was such terrible news, and I couldn't communicate well with the family in Spanish.

When I walked into the room, I remember seeing Irasema in bed. She had been placed in a drug-induced coma. There were tubes everywhere as they tried to keep her alive. Her mom held Irasema's hand, and she had tears flowing down her cheeks. Her dad sat in the corner in shock, trying to understand the terrible news they had just received. What could I do here? Nothing. I was focused on what I could or could not do. Jesús helped me converse with the parents for a little bit. I told them that when they were ready, I could anoint Irasema. Her mother had a strong faith. I could see that she truly believed in the healing power of the sacrament. We prayed, and I anointed Irasema. We exchanged phone numbers, and I told them to call me at any time. Jesús and I left shortly after we celebrated the sacrament. I expected that I would be receiving a call in the coming days to plan her funeral. Oh, you of little faith!

About a week to ten days passed, and I still hadn't heard from Irasema's parents. I finally called her mom and asked how Irasema was doing. She was overjoyed on the phone and full of hope. She said, "Fr. Burke, Irasema's getting better, and the doctors can't explain it!" The hair on my neck stood on end as she told me the news. After the phone call, I fell to my knees in tears.

The healing continued to happen. Irasema kept getting better. After a while, she was released from the hospital and went home. She was in a wheelchair, but eventually she was back to walking. Three years later we celebrated Irasema's quinceañera, her fifteenth birthday. Now she's a young woman; she is not without health concerns, but the fact that she is alive is a miracle that can only be attributed to God. When I visit the family in West Chicago, her mom wants to canonize me. I tell her, "It was your faith that healed her. Honestly, I was doubting, but you had the faith that I didn't have."

In Scripture, Jesus often told people, "Your faith has saved you." Through this experience, Jesus was taking me by the hand like a little boy, saying, "Burke, do you trust me? I am alive. I am working in the sacraments." Now, do I see people healed all the time from physical ailments? No. I've had a few of those experiences. But even when there is no physical healing, there is always deep spiritual healing when I celebrate the sacrament of the Anointing of the Sick. Since that experience with Irasema early in my priesthood, I have never celebrated a sacrament doubting that God is at work. I may not see the results myself, but I know that he is sending his grace. And he asks, "Do you trust me, Burke? Do you believe?" My answer will forever be yes.

* * *

In the spring of 2006, I received a phone call from Bishop Imesch asking me if I'd be interested in becoming the new vocation director for the Diocese of Joliet. It would mean that I would be the main promoter of the priesthood in the diocese. I would oversee the selection process of the seminarians, and I would walk with the seminarians through their formation process. Bishop Sartain had already been named the new Bishop of Joliet, but since he didn't know the priests of our diocese, he asked Bishop Imesch to appoint someone. I happily said yes to the request, as I trusted that the Holy Spirit speaks through the bishops. With a new assignment starting in a few months, I had to start the process of saying goodbye to the people of St. Mary's in West Chicago.

For my last Mass at St. Mary's, we had an outdoor bilingual celebration because we couldn't fit everyone in the church. It was a small church, but it was a big community. We celebrated nine to ten Masses every weekend in order to serve all the people. It was a very emotional day for me. After four years, as I looked around the congregation, I knew everybody's story: I buried her mother; I counseled them in their marriage; I baptized their kids; I witnessed the marriage of their son and daughter-in-law; he struggled with drugs at one time. How intimately I had become involved in all their lives!

It was extremely difficult to leave West Chicago, but I reflected on the mission of Jesus in Scripture. He'd go from village to village preaching. They'd want him to stay, but he had to keep on moving. As priests, we are called to follow the mission of Jesus and go where we are sent. This is not always easy, but it is a necessary part of ministry. For some priests, leaving a parish feels like a death. It is so painful that they begin to build walls around their hearts so that they can never hurt like that again.

Pain is always involved when we love and have to move on. I see that poignantly when a spouse has to bury the love of their life. We priests are called to love the people in our parishes. After a period of time, we are called to move on to love another community. A few people become lifelong friends—like Jesús Fernandez—and you keep in touch. Everyone else still holds a special place in your heart, but you have to make more room in your heart for the new community you are called to serve.

When we love, the Church becomes fully alive. A parish takes on a lot of the characteristics of its priests. If the pastor is loving and giving, the parish will become loving and giving. You get what you give. I went from wanting to leave St. Mary's in the first few months to not wanting to leave at all. My four years at St. Mary's shaped me into the priest I am today, gave me lasting friendships, and prepared me for the next chapter of my life as vocation director for the Diocese of Joliet.

CHAPTER NINE

SEARCHING FOR MY IDENTITY

As adults, we easily let our career become our identity and our validation for success. Even when we have a strong faith, our world tells us that our identity comes from our mission, career, job, and income. We project to others that we are successful, even when we feel empty inside. Throughout the time I played baseball, my identity and my self-worth were directly related to how I performed on the baseball field. I was so focused on who I was as a baseball player that after my playing days were over, I had an identity crisis. I didn't know who I was.

I clung to my perfectionistic tendencies to prove to myself and others that I was worth something. I hoped others would like the "perfect" Burke that I tried to project to the world. I based my identity on what people thought of me, which is a slippery slope. I believed the lie that I had to be perfect in every way for God and people to love me. I didn't think I could be loved by anyone because I didn't love myself. I hated my shortcomings; in my mind, they made me unlovable. But our humanity is not perfect; it's flawed.

In seminary, they told us that our fundamental identity was a beloved son of God. I constantly took this idea to prayer. I desired to believe that I was a beloved son of God, but I didn't think it was possible. How could God love me, with all my imperfections and sinfulness? I knew myself too well and focused on what was wrong with me. I could not see my value as a beloved son of God, created in his image and likeness.

One day, as I was praying about my identity in Christ, I saw myself climbing a ladder to heaven. This imaginative prayer experience was so powerful for me that it remains as clear to me today as the day when it happened. God's grace continues to flow from this vision. In my prayer, as I climbed the ladder, I noticed that the higher I climbed and the harder I toiled, the taller the ladder got and the further heaven moved away from me. It was exhausting work.

From far below me, a voice cried out, "Burke, let go!" I looked down and Jesus stood at the base of the ladder with his arms open wide. "Burke," he said again, "let go!" His smile and open arms were so inviting, but I was not ready to let go.

"No," I said, "I got this!" It was as if to say, "I'm in control. I can do this!" In my stubbornness, I pushed even harder, hand over hand, rung after rung, but all I did was wear out my arms. No matter how hard I tried, heaven was always out of reach. I thought I had to do it all by myself, but it was exactly my self-reliance that kept me from moving any higher. "Trust me," Jesus said gently, as he extended his arms further as a sign of invitation.

Tired and shaking, I took a deep breath and leaned back off the ladder with my arms open wide. It was like the old commercial of the "Nestea Plunge." The ladder rushed by as I fell, and then in my prayer, Jesus caught me. It was the five-year-old Burke that was caught in the arms of Jesus. Our eyes met, and I was filled with an overwhelming sense of God's love and freedom. As Jesus gazed upon me with compassion, I felt pure joy, relief, and peace. I suddenly realized that I didn't have to climb the ladder any longer, which was exhausting in the first place. Jesus was teaching me that I only had to surrender to him, and he would do the rest. He wanted to release me from the burden of my self-reliance and from the pressure I put on myself to achieve and to be perfect. I thought those were the things that would bring me acceptance, love, and maybe heaven. He set me free from that burden and showed me my job was to surrender to his loving embrace and gaze.

I would love to say that I am completely free from perfectionism, self-reliance, and seeking worldly validation of my identity. Although I have made great strides in believing that I am a beloved son of God, it's something that will probably continue to deepen the rest of my life. Receiving healing and freedom is a lifelong journey for all of us. Jesus, in his kindness, meets us where we are and heals us when we are ready. It is like an onion. Each time a layer gets pulled back, the Lord's grace-filled touch goes deeper. I have received great healing through that vision of Jesus and the ladder. Pope St. John Paul II once said, "We are not the sum of our weaknesses and failures; we are the sum of the Father's love for us and our real capacity to become the image of his Son." It took me a long time to accept that, but now it's a fundamental part of who I am and how I view myself. The more I prayed and allowed God's love to enter in, the more I realized that I am a beloved son. It helped me root my identity in God and worry less about what other people thought of me.

Now when I preach on retreats, I focus on identity as the number one theme. I say to attendees, "What is your fundamental identity? You are a beloved son or daughter of God, and that will never change. Your economic status, your job, and your earthly relationships all might change, but God will always love you because you are his child. You never have to earn his love." I love to see this truth sink into the hearts of people for the first time, especially someone who has believed the lie their whole life that they are unworthy of the love of God. Our only job is to surrender to God and let him love us, gaze upon us, and delight in us. This truth is life changing. It is revolutionary. It is freeing.

* * *

As much as I tried to stay rooted in my identity as a child of God, there were times in my new position as the vocation director that I struggled. One of the joys was moving back to Joliet and living close to Dad and Jan. When I started as vocation director in 2006, the diocese had twenty-four seminarians. As success of a vocation director is often defined by the numbers, I was tempted to get my identity from how many seminarians we had. Every time I ran into brother priests, before asking me how I was, they asked how many seminarians we had. I really had to fight against focusing on numbers. And I have always been a numbers guy!

I probably made some mistakes during my first couple of years in this new position. I had to remind myself and pray that I could let go of the lie that my success was defined by the number of seminarians we had. If I did what God asked of me each day, I could count that as a success. During my twelve years as vocation director, we saw the numbers increase dramatically, thanks be to God. But I did not base my identity on them. I attributed the increase in seminarians to the work of the Holy Spirit. I am proud of these men like a father would be, but I am grounded in my sonship of our heavenly Father. That truth will never change. The number of seminarians changes every year, but my fundamental identity remains the same.

I am so grateful for the twelve people that comprised the vocation team, who helped me during the dozen years I worked as vocation director. This group assisted me with interviews and advised me on all our seminarians. The team included priests, deacons, religious sisters, and lay men and women from different backgrounds, including doctors and psychologists. Our goal was to raise the bar very high for new seminarians. You might think that the numbers would decrease due to higher standards, but they increased. Good men drew other good men into the seminary as they pictured themselves ministering side by side in the diocese.

I aimed to inform people around the diocese about vocations so often that they would consider it a normal part of life. I wanted every family to raise their children with the question "What is God's plan for my life?" We had seminarians speak after Communion at parish Masses, play basketball against school teams, participate in youth events, and be present at our Catholic sports camps. I wanted families to see that these talented seminarians could have done many things with their lives, but they had chosen to follow God's call to be a priest. And I wanted every Catholic young man and woman to consider the priesthood and religious life as well marriage and single life. I took it as a compliment when people told me they had heard more about vocations from me than they had in their lifetime.

Because of the priest abuse scandal in 2002, we had to look closely at the process for admitting candidates. We lengthened the application with more detailed questions, expanded the vocation team, adapted the interviews, and enhanced the psychological exam. No system will completely prevent someone with bad intentions from entering the seminary, but the Church today is doing everything possible to protect our young and vulnerable people.

Once an application was received, we had three people on the team interview the candidate. They reported back to the team of twelve. Together we considered the interview results and then voted on each candidate. The team listened closely to the Holy Spirit while respecting the dignity of each man that applied. I especially valued the input that the women brought to the team because they sense things that men do not. I also wanted to know how well the candidates treated women. If my secretary said that a young man was rude or disrespectful, that was a big strike against him. Women make up the majority of parish staffs and congregations, and we cannot tolerate any disrespectful treatment.

I trusted every member of our vocation team and valued their input. We considered each candidate with the questions: Would I want this applicant as my pastor? Would I want this man to minister to my parents? Would I want my children to grow up with this priest as their role model? Our team represented the voice of the Church, discerning whether or not this man had a call from God. One team member always asked the group, "Would I want this man to marry my daughter?" If the answer was no, we did not want him to marry the Church as a priest.

My hardest task as vocation director was telling a seminarian that he could not continue in formation. My second-hardest task was telling a man that he could not begin seminary training, especially if it was his lifelong dream. I wouldn't give applications to men unless I felt strongly that they would be accepted. It was easier to tell them in advance that the priesthood was probably not their vocation than it was to tell a seminarian that he needed to leave formation. It's like an engaged couple calling off their wedding; it's better to end the relationship before the wedding than afterward.

I do not like conflict. Having to let a seminarian go or dealing with a difficult situation used to cause my stomach to churn. But the position taught me that to be a spiritual father, I needed to learn how to discipline and prepare men to be good fathers themselves. When I was first named vocation director in 2006, I was thirty-nine years old and saw myself as the seminarians' older brother. After some years in the office, there came a time when I was older than the parents of the seminarians. As I grew in my identity as a beloved son of God, I learned what it meant to become a spiritual father, and I called seminarians to greatness and challenged them like a father challenges his children.

I talked with Nashville Dominican Sister Cecelia Joseph, an original member of my vocation team, about my hesitancy to call out seminarians for their behavior. She explained that I shouldn't look at it as calling them out, but instead as calling them up. Jesus always called people up. He met people where they were, loved them without condemnation, and then called them to greatness or holiness. Sister said that the guys knew I loved them, but a good father would do what was right for their son no matter how difficult or painful it would seem at first. If I ever had a doubt, Bishop Sartain had advised me that I should err on the side of the Church. In other words, if we had questions about whether a seminarian should continue, we should err on the side of asking them to leave the seminary because there was so much at stake through their priesthood. I recognized that these men would have a great influence on thousands of people. If they were not ready to take the responsibility seriously as beloved sons, chaste spouses, and spiritual fathers, then they should not become priests.

* * *

Recent studies have shown that parents are the biggest obstacle to vocations to the priesthood or religious life. Once a mother made an appointment to see me. She said, "Over my dead body will my daughter become a religious sister." I asked her more about why she felt this way.

She said, "I have dreams for us. We are going to go shopping together. I am going to babysit her children." She went on and on about the plans she had for her daughter and their future life.

"I hear what you want," I asked, "but what about your daughter? What if God is calling her to be a religious sister?"

Eventually, the mother admitted that she wanted her daughter to be happy and that happiness would come in following God's will. She left my office a little more at peace but still hoping that her daughter would choose to get married and have children.

About four years later, I was visiting Mundelein for an event. A young religious sister in full habit came running up to me and said, "Fr. Burke, do you know who I am?"

I didn't recognize her and shook my head no.

She said, "My mother was in your office a few years ago and you helped her accept my vocation."

I asked, "Is your mother still alive?" (Recalling that she had said, "Over my dead body will my daughter become a religious sister.")

The young sister said with a smile, "Oh yes, she's alive. She sees how happy I am as a sister, and she has embraced my vocation."

That made my day! It brought me back to my conversation with my dad when I first told him I felt the call to priesthood. He asked me if I could be happy being a priest and not being married. I asked him how he knew Mom was the one for him. He said, "I just knew." When I found my calling to be a priest, *I just knew*, and it led to true happiness and fulfillment—though not without some heavy crosses.

I am convinced, through my experience and through working with hundreds of young people, that the way to find true happiness is discerning the will of God and following his plan. It was beautiful to watch many parents change their views once their son was in seminary for a year or two. If the priesthood was their son's vocation, they became the person God created them to be and became fully alive. As St. Irenaeus said, "The glory of God is a human being fully alive." Once they saw the joy in their sons, some parents who had expressed their strong resistance to their sons going to seminary offered to talk to other parents struggling with their sons' decision. "I'll go speak with them," they said, "because we've seen our son come alive as he followed his call." Early in my time in the vocations office, we began a group called POPS (Parents of Priests and Seminarians). It was a support group for parents who have sons who are priests or are in the seminary. POPS has helped parents share their fears and desires with one another, and it gave me the opportunity to shepherd them on the journey as well. My biggest advice to the parents was to give their sons true freedom to discern. They should not ordain them the first day they enter seminary, and they should not push them out of seminary. Their sons needed the freedom to discern whether God was calling them to this vocation.

* * *

As vocation director, I had the wonderful opportunity to guide many young men into their priestly vocations. Let me tell you one such story. The first time I met Mark, I was speaking at his parish about vocations. After Mass, I noticed a young man cautiously waiting off to the side, and I knew he wanted to talk. When I finished greeting all the people after Mass, he slowly approached me.

"Father, I've been Catholic my whole life," he said, "but I am going to a Protestant university. We go to chapel a few times a week. And some of the things they teach are very different from what the Catholic Church believes. And I am very confused."

He paused.

"I am thinking about leaving the Church."

"Well, before you leave the Church," I said, "make sure you get to know her."

I invited Mark to a young adult group called Spirit and Truth that met every week. We'd begin each evening with thirty to forty-five minutes of Church teaching. Then we'd spend time in Adoration with some praise and worship music, and we'd close with some social time.

Mark and his sister came every week. He learned more about the faith and spent more time before the Blessed Sacrament. He grew tremendously in his faith.

A few years later, I recommended Mark to FOCUS (the Fellowship of Catholic University Students). They had called me looking for faith-filled young men to serve as missionaries on college campuses. They contacted Mark and interviewed him right away, and they assigned him as a FOCUS missionary for two years.

Mark and I kept in touch while he served on a college campus in Omaha. We talked periodically during his time as a missionary.

"Father, I have a girlfriend and feel called to marriage," Mark told me on one phone call, "but I am also feeling a call to the priesthood."

We spoke a lot about vocations over Mark's two years as a missionary, and he discerned that he should pursue the priesthood. I recommended that he come back to Joliet to join the seminary. Mark completed the first two years of pre-theology and four years of theology, and he was ordained in 2017. Now Fr. Mark is a pastor. I had the opportunity to live with him in his parish while I was serving as the Director of Adult Formation for the diocese. Walking with him from the point when he said, "Father I am leaving the Church," to working with him in the same parish has been rewarding. He is doing great things for the Lord.

I learned the important role of a vocation director in discipling seminarians and accompanying them on their journey. Yes, there is decision-making along the way, but I tried to facilitate their relationship with the Lord and walk with them. Jesus is their ultimate vocation director with the Holy Spirit guiding the way.

* * *

One of the first events I attended as vocation director was an Andrew Dinner. It was named after St. Andrew, who met Jesus and then brought his brother Peter to meet him. Priests brought young men to this dinner to meet the bishop and open the door for conversations about religious vocations. At my first Andrew Dinner with Bishop Sartain, a young man asked me, "Do you ever get lonely as a priest?" I was surprised by the question. I thought about the difficult transition I experienced from parish life, where I was intimately involved in the lives of many people, to being the vocation director, which was very different from serving in a parish. I had a period of adjustment and loneliness while I was figuring out my new role.

When the young man asked me if I experienced loneliness, I had this internal conversation: "If I say no, I'm lying, and I can't lie. If I say yes, which is true, how can I promote the priesthood?" For some reason, I thought that priests and religious experienced loneliness, but not married people.

Bishop Sartain saw me struggling with the question and came to my rescue. "Sure, we get lonely," he said, "but so do your parents, single people, and religious people. Loneliness is part of the human condition. God made us with a longing in our heart that only he can fill." Then he said this line that changed my spiritual life: "Loneliness is God's invitation to intimacy with him."

I was relieved to hear that I was not the only one and that priesthood was not the only vocation that experienced loneliness. I had never thought loneliness was an invitation to intimacy with God. When I felt lonely before that conversation, I turned on a ball game or called a friend, which were not bad things to do. But those things were not what my heart sought; my heart longed for God. When you get hungry, your body is telling you that it wants food. What do you eat? If you eat junk food every time you get hungry, your body will slow down and eventually fall apart. When we experience loneliness, our soul is saying, "I'm hungry! I'm hungry for God!" If we only give our soul spiritual junk food every time we get lonely, it's going to shrivel up.

I share that spiritual truth with as many people as I can. It resonates with every person with whom I share it. I no longer run from the feeling of loneliness. I also no longer try to fill the void with things that never satisfy. I turn to prayer. I feed my soul by spending quiet time with God. Only after prayer do I call my friends or watch a ball game. When I get lonely, I know God is saying to me, "I'm the one for whom you are looking. Make me the priority in your life." It's another reminder that I draw my identity from God first.

For my first five years as vocation director, I lived at the Fiat House in downtown Joliet. I had the wonderful opportunity to live with Fr. Jim Lennon, who had just retired. He was one of the most respected priests in the diocese and a great mentor. We prayed Morning and Evening Prayer and Mass together. Sometimes I got up early to pray, and Fr. Jim would already be in the chapel praying. Other times I would get home late from a long day of work, and he'd be in the chapel praying. He modeled for me the connection between prayer and joy in any vocation. Fr. Jim passed away on May 8, 2022. God rest his soul.

Studies done by secular groups list the priesthood as the happiest "career." But the priesthood is not a career. A vocation is a way of life, a way of being; a career is something that we do. The priesthood should be compared more to other vocations like marriage, single life, and religious life. Still, I think that it's ranked as one of the happiest careers because it has so much meaning. There were days when I worked as an actuary that I did not want to get out of bed. I dreaded the monotony of the job, and I felt that my work didn't matter in the big picture of life. I always wanted my life to make a difference. There has never been a day when I dreaded getting out of bed as a priest. I wake up and offer my day to God. "Ok, Lord, let's do this," I pray. I trust that he is going to give me the grace to speak and act in every situation. Celebrating the sacraments and having authentic encounters with people at the most important times of their lives convinces me that what I do each day can have an eternal impact on them.

* * *

The morning after Dennis and I were ordained, we were talking before our first Masses. We could not believe what had transpired the day before. At one point, Dennis stopped, looked down at his hands, and said, "Wow, I'm a priest!" In subsequent summers after our ordination, Dennis and I started teaching a one-week class at the Institute of Priestly Formation. The IPF summer program had a huge impact on us as seminarians and priests. We were happy to go back as priests to pass along what we had learned. We taught the five identities of diocesan priests: Beloved Son, Chaste Spouse, Spiritual Father, Divine Physician, and Head and Shepherd. Jesus lived these identities, and priests are called to participate in these identities of Jesus. Teaching these valuable concepts to seminarians at the IPF prepared me for my role as vocation director. I have formed hundreds of young men in these identities of the priest. I want to say more about them.

Beloved Son. Knowing that we are a beloved son (or daughter) of our heavenly Father is the fundamental identity from which all other identities flow. At his baptism, Jesus heard the Father say, "This is my Son, the Beloved, with whom I am well pleased" (Matt. 3:17). And at our Baptism, we become children of God and grow in this identity throughout our lives. We can't give ourselves away in love to anyone if we don't first know that we are loved unconditionally by God. We can't give what we don't have.

Chaste Spouse. As a man matures as a child of God, he can give himself away in love to a spouse, either to a woman in marriage or to the Church as a priest. As celibate men, priests are not bachelors. A bachelor thinks only about himself and does whatever he wants to do. As a priest, I am a faithful spouse to the Church, and I'm called to lay down my life for my spouse as Jesus did on the cross and as a husband does for his wife.

Spiritual Father. The priest is a spiritual father called to love and nurture his spiritual children just as a man and wife love and nurture their children. A man does not take on the priesthood for eight hours a day. He's on all the time. It is who you are, not what you do, like the father of a family. If someone from his family needs him, he takes care of them. My dad taught me what it means to be responsible for a family. He worked hard to support us, and he was present to us as fully as possible.

Divine Physician. Healing was an integral part of Jesus' ministry. He healed the sick, the blind, and the lame. His heart was moved with pity as people brought the sick to him. A priest lives out his identity as a spiritual physician by uniting himself to Jesus the healer. I have witnessed beautiful physical, spiritual, and emotional healings, especially through the sacraments. In Joliet, we hold healing retreats, based on Dr. Bob Schuchts' book *Be Healed*, where people receive healing from their wounds. I never imagined myself as a part of a healing ministry, but I realize that since it's important to Jesus, it must be important to me as a priest.

Head and Shepherd. Jesus' mission is to return to the Father all that the Father has given him. I take this identity very seriously. A priest is a shepherd who gets to know his sheep and the sound of their cry. His goal is to bring them safely back to the Father. Pope Francis says that we need to smell like our sheep. Priests need to spend quality time with the people that we serve in order to know their needs, meet them where they are, share the love of God with them, and shepherd them to heaven—all with the help of God's grace.

Teaching this course allowed me to reflect on the identities of my own priesthood and inspired me to live them out fully. And during my twelve years as vocation director, I had to look in the mirror constantly because I was a spiritual father to these young men. I had to reflect on my own priesthood so that I could be an example for the seminarians. I could not expect them to do anything that I was not living out myself. If I was to mentor these young men, I needed to live a life of authenticity and integrity.

* * *

One of my favorite days of the year is ordination day. As I mentioned earlier, I had to grow from seeing myself as a spiritual brother to the seminarians to seeing myself as a spiritual father. As time passed, the identity of being a spiritual father became more natural for me. At our monthly POPS meetings, I told the parents that I saw myself as another father to their children. On ordination day, when the seminarians became brother priests, I always had a great sense of emotion and joy. During the Mass, I could recall when I first met them, when they first started seminary, when they struggled, and when they triumphed. I imagine parents have the same feelings when their children get married.

What I enjoyed most about being a vocation director was building relationships with the men and their families. I met some of our priests when they were still in middle school. It was a joy to see them mature and grow through the years. At every ordination, I still cry tears of joy as my spiritual sons begin this new chapter of their lives.

Statistics say the highest burnout rate among priests is among vocation directors. There are a couple of reasons for this. Vocation directors do not always have a community like parish priests do, and they often feel the pressure of producing numbers for the diocese. To stay healthy in any position as priests, we need to have different levels of relationships—family, friends, and brother priests. My family has been supportive every step of the way. They remain my rock, and they keep me accountable and humble.

I am grateful for the amazing friends God has brought me. He placed certain people in my life at the exact moment I needed them to keep me going, and they remain my friends. By surrounding myself with these great friends, I felt that I was staying healthy and had a lot of energy for the ministry. Many of them are lay people. Our vocations complement one another, and they keep me grounded.

I have also been blessed to be part of a priest support group. We meet every month to share what's happening, both in our personal and public lives. We have supported one another through some difficult experiences. We know our brothers have our backs, and that's so important.

In the last ten years, I have become more involved in the Cursillo movement that helps men and women grow in holiness. Parents who draw closer to Christ on a Cursillo learn to draw their children closer to him. Vocations come from holy families. We also developed a strong men's ministry called the Fishers of Men. We encourage men to gather weekly in small groups, monthly at our Catholic Man Nights, and annually at our men's conference. These events encourage men to take their role as husbands and fathers seriously. In order to increase vocations, it's important to think long term and focus on the family. If we help families to grow in holiness, vocations to the priesthood and religious life will flourish, as well as holy vocations to the married and single life.

Working as the vocation director allowed me to see how much the bishop does for our diocese. When I came to work in the chancery for the diocese in 2006, I was put on the Curia Council, a group of nine who met twice a month to advise the bishop. My involvement with the diocese has led some people to ask me interesting questions like "What are your goals? Do you want to be a bishop? Or pope?" From a secular point of view, people think I want to become a bishop, like climbing the corporate ladder. I just want to do God's will. I love living in the moment where God has me right now.

I have done things I never dreamed of, like going on mission trips to Bolivia, the Philippines, and Guatemala and leading pilgrimages to Mexico, Italy, the Holy Land, Spain, France, and Australia. If we earnestly seek God's will with an open heart and mind, he blesses us abundantly in ways we never thought possible. If you want to make God laugh, tell him your plans. If somebody had asked me before I got ordained to dream my wildest dreams, I would not have been able to imagine all the people that I have met, all the amazing experiences I have had with the faithful, or all the travel to different parts of the world. It's been incredible!

I had planned to become a professional baseball player, make millions of dollars, and have a big family. God had different plans. He said to me, "Burke, I have more in store for you than you ever imagined. Your family will be gigantic. You will be rich in graces. You will have the opportunity to impact the eternal lives of thousands of people. You will be a Major League Catholic priest."

You cannot outdo God in generosity. I dare you to try!

CHAPTER TEN

A GRAND SLAM FOR GOD

The night before I was ordained, I was praying in the cathedral, preparing myself for the day that would change my life forever. I was excited and nervous at the same time. I had left so much behind. I wasn't doubting the priesthood, but I was having a hard time understanding why God had placed some things in my life only to have me give them up.

"God," I prayed, "I've given up Stephanie, who I thought I would marry. I've given up having a family. I've given up baseball. I've given up every dream I had to follow you. What's in it for me?" I felt like St. Peter when he said to the Lord, "We have given up everything and followed you. What will there be for us?" (Matt. 19:27). Behind these questions was a lack of trust in the Lord. I wondered if I could be happy as a priest. Would I regret giving up everything? I didn't get an answer to my prayer. God simply replied, "Trust me."

I did trust him, and I was ordained June 1, 2002. In November of that same year, I celebrated the wedding of Stephanie and Matt. It was held at Holy Cross in Batavia, Illinois, where all three of us had met. God had a good laugh, because when I prayed about not getting to marry Stephanie, he knew that I'd get to marry her anyway, just as a priest. That I never felt jealous was even more beautiful. As Matt and Stephanie exchanged their vows, I couldn't believe how happy I was for them to marry and how happy I was as a priest. It reminded me that the way to find happiness is doing the will of God. The three of us could not have planned how our lives turned out; it was all in God's design. Stephanie and Matt might not have met if I hadn't dated her. Now they're really happy and have three children, each of whom I had the honor of baptizing.

When I reflect on their wedding day, I have no regrets. Do I think I could have married Stephanie and been happy? Absolutely. But I know that God created me to be a priest. Priesthood is the path by which I would find the deepest fulfillment, joy, and peace. Many people have not included God in the discernment of their vocation, and they live a restless life. Following God's will does not mean everything will be perfect. There are crosses in every vocation, but the Lord gives the grace to carry the crosses along the way.

I remain great friends with Matt and Stephanie. We celebrate together the milestones of their lives and of their children's lives. God continues to return to me everything that I had given up. He has shown me that I hadn't lost any of my dreams. His dreams were so much bigger than mine. What I didn't know was how God would bring baseball back into my life.

* * *

In 2012, I attended the National Conference for Diocesan Vocation Directors, which I tried to attend every year. It's an opportunity for vocation directors from around the country to gather, share best practices, learn from one another, and enjoy fraternity. That year I met Fr. J.D. Jaffe, the vocation director for the Diocese of Arlington, Virginia. When he heard about my background in baseball, he said that I needed to meet Ray McKenna. He told me that Ray was the founder of the Catholic Athletes for Christ and that he connected priests as chaplains with Major League teams. Instantly, my interest was piqued. Fr. Jaffe promised to give Ray my phone number when he returned home. Ray also lived in the Arlington diocese. Sure enough, Ray McKenna called me a few days after I returned home.

"Fr. Burke," he said, "Fr. Jaffe told me about your history and that you live in the Chicago area. Well, we're in need of a Catholic chaplain for the Chicago . . ." There seemed like a long pause, and then he said "Cubs." God really does have a sense of humor. I was hoping that Ray would say "White Sox." Don't get me wrong: I was excited for the opportunity. But I was raised to hate the Cubs! My parents and oldest brother Brock were diehard St. Louis Cardinals fans. Blaine had become a Cincinnati Reds fan, and I became a Philadelphia Phillies fan after watching Mike Schmidt hit three home runs against the Cubs one day. The Cardinals and Cubs are fierce rivals. And so are the Cubs and the White Sox. I was on the opposite side of the Cubs in both rivalries. I could imagine my mother rolling over in her grave knowing that I was going to be the chaplain for the Chicago Cubs! All joking aside, I could not believe I was getting another chance to be in the Major Leagues. With a laugh at God's sense of humor, I accepted the volunteer position.

The spring of 2013 marked my first season with the Cubs. As far as I knew, they had never had a Catholic priest as a regular chaplain before. Every Sunday home game, I drove to Wrigley Field and celebrated Mass for players or employees from the Cubs and the visiting team that wanted to attend. There was no chapel in Wrigley Field, so to celebrate Mass we were given the Cubs' family room, where the wives and kids of the players hung out during games.

At the first Mass I celebrated, the only ones there were me and Shawn Camp, a pitcher for the Cubs and a recent convert to Catholicism. I wondered what I was doing there. It was an hour drive from my house to Wrigley Field. Was it worth it to celebrate Mass for one person? I took a deep breath. It was okay. I reminded myself that great things often start very small. I knew that God had a plan, and I intended to do my best. After that first Mass, I put signs up in Wrigley Field where the employees and the players would see them. Slowly, people started to find out that Mass was available to them at the stadium. This was a great service for them because they often had to work Saturday evening until very late and then be back at the stadium very early for a Sunday afternoon game. More Cubs employees and players and some from the visiting team began to attend.

By the end of the season, the number at Mass had risen to about twenty. After Mass each Sunday, I went to the locker room to speak to the players and ask for any prayer intentions they might have. As is true in any ministry, it was a matter of building relationships and trust to lay a strong foundation. I looked forward to the next season and to continue combining my love for baseball and my love for God. It was a perfect match for me to bring my passions together. I continued my full-time work as the diocesan vocation director while serving as chaplain for the Cubs twice a month at Sunday home games.

* * *

In November 2013, I flew to California for the Catholic Athletes for Christ retreat. It is an annual retreat for Minor League, Major League, and retired ball players and the priest chaplains around the country. There was time for Mass, spiritual talks, prayer, and fellowship. At the retreat, I met Mike Sweeney for the first time. He was a five-time all-star for the Kansas City Royals over a career of sixteen years and was inducted into the Royals Hall of Fame in 2015. Mike was unashamedly Catholic and was known for not being afraid to share his faith publicly. When I met him, I thought, "No one can be this nice and positive all the time." Getting to know him over the years, I can say that Mike Sweeney is one of the most genuine, positive, on-fire Catholics I have ever met. He has become one of my dearest friends. We now hold each other accountable in our walk with Christ and encourage one another to be saints.

Mike is the second of seven children in a very Catholic family. When he was born, he had a fifty-fifty chance that he would survive the first day. His mom asked the Blessed Mother to intercede for him. When Mike survived, she dedicated him to Mary. In a spirit of thanksgiving, Mike has always had a strong devotion to her. At his Confirmation retreat at fourteen, Mike had a deep encounter with Jesus, and he dedicated himself to serving the Lord for the rest of his life.

A superb baseball player, the Kansas City Royals drafted Mike right out of high school. He was a teenager going out into the world. The faith that his parents handed on to him was his foundation in this new world of Minor League Baseball. He continued to attend Mass weekly when many of his teammates were not giving a second thought to God. Mike worked hard and overcame a lot of obstacles. He was drafted in 1991 and made his MLB debut in 1995. The early years were not easy. At one point, one of the coaches told Mike, "You have a zero percent chance of making this team." But he ended up having a fifteen-year Major League career, mostly with the Kansas City Royals.

Mike was known as one of the best teammates in Major League Baseball. He was intense, passionate, and hardworking, and he cared intensely about people. He incorporated his faith into everything that he did. He has probably done more for the Catholic Church than any athlete in any sport. Mike is, and always has been, very public about what he believes. He is a husband and a father of six. He takes seriously his role to help his family get to heaven. They pray as a family and go to Mass almost every day. He is bold in his life and in his faith.

Mike told me the incredible story of his Catholic Baseball Camps. He said God had inspired him to "tell the greatest story ever told with the greatest game ever played" by sharing the story of Jesus Christ though baseball. As he shared his idea of starting a

Catholic baseball camp, people told him that no one would attend a Catholic camp. They said he should make it a Christian camp so more people might come. Mike said that even if he got only ten kids, it would be a great time, and they'd raise up ten saints. One hundred and fifty kids from all over the country attended the first camp in Kansas City. God had called Mike to express his faith in this unique way, and people responded to it. He also hosted camps in San Diego and Seattle, both with amazing turnouts.

In the summer of 2014, Mike invited me to the baseball camp in Seattle. I was blown away by what I experienced. The boys and girls and the coaches started each day with Mass at 8 a.m. For the rest of the morning, the kids received small group instruction at rotating stations. After lunch, a couple men shared their faith testimonies, and the kids played fun scrimmage games in the afternoon. The games had twists, like the "Silent Second," where the kids couldn't make a sound during the second inning or they would have to do ten pushups. Each inning taught something about the faith. For example, the silent second inning was a reminder that we need to curb our tongue and learn not to say everything that comes to mind. In the "Backward Fourth," the players had to run to third base instead of first. Sometimes we have to learn to retrain our minds to go against some of our bad habits.

At the end of the day, players and coaches gathered to affirm the kids that were exemplary in virtue that day. For example, if someone stopped to help a teammate who was struggling, the player who helped was lauded in front of the entire group. This daily activity built an environment of virtue and encouragement. Mike gave a talk on Mary and prayed part of the Rosary with the kids. Then he taught them about God's mercy.

Afterward, the kids had the opportunity to go to confession right on the baseball field. Priests were stationed on each of the bases and the pitcher's mound. After Mike explained the beauty of the sacrament of Reconciliation, the kids literally ran onto the field for confession. The whole program was a wonderful way to evangelize and share Christ's love through baseball. I knew I had to bring it back to Joliet.

Over a hundred kids attended our first Mike Sweeney Catholic Baseball Camp at Providence Catholic High School in July 2015 in New Lenox, Illinois. We have hosted the camp every summer since then, except in 2020, when we had to cancel due to the coronavirus. Mike usually comes to the camp for a day to meet the kids and their families and to share his testimony with them. Each year, families from all over the country attend our camp, although a majority are from the Diocese of Joliet.

One summer, a family came from Taiwan to attend one of Mike's camps. The boys' mom said that there was nothing like it in Taiwan. She said, "We can go to baseball camps anywhere, but I've never seen one combine our Catholic faith with the fundamentals of the game." Mike has had entire families convert to the Catholic faith after attending one of his camps. We had a thirteen-year-old ask to be baptized because of the camp and the role models he encountered there.

The baseball camp became so popular that we added a Catholic soccer camp. One of our seminarians coordinated it with Fr. Chase Hilgenbrink, who was a professional soccer player before he became a priest for the Diocese of Peoria, Illinois. We also started a Spirit Hockey Camp that features Bishop Paprocki from Springfield, Illinois, who wrote the book *Holy Goalies for Body and Soul.* Most recently we added Catholic basketball and football camps as well.*

Mike Sweeney has taught me to be bold in my faith. He prays regularly with his wife and children at home. I was out to dinner with him and other ball players during spring training, and we prayed part of the Rosary in the restaurant. When we finished praying, an elderly man came over to the table and said, "Thank you for being bold to pray in public. I am eighty-one years old,

---

* You can find more information at www.catholicsportscamps.org.

and I recently became Catholic because of men like you." Wow! I have been so encouraged by Mike's boldness to speak about his faith and pray in public. He is not afraid of what people may think about him. I can see the fruits of Mike's "yes" to God's call. He has impacted the lives of so many people around the country and world.

* * *

The Cubs began renovating Wrigley Field after the 2014 season, and they tore out the family room where I had been celebrating Mass. That we no longer had a chapel didn't stop Christ from coming to Wrigley. Like Mary and Joseph who couldn't find a room to have their baby, we looked all over Wrigley Field for a proper place to celebrate Mass. With approval, we decided to celebrate Mass out in the seats on the third base line. The people call it the "Cathedral of Wrigley Field." As I celebrate Mass, tours are going on around us, forklifts are carrying supplies to the concession stands, and airplanes are flying overhead, but more people are attending Mass regularly. God's hand is at work in this ministry.

At the start of the 2015 season, Joe Maddon joined the team as the new manager of the Cubs. One of the things that quickly impressed me about Joe was that he treated everyone the same. It didn't matter if you were the best player on the team or the college intern on the grounds crew. Everyone was important in his eyes. He was very welcoming to me, and he said he liked my presence at Wrigley because it changed the environment in the locker room and on the field. Maddon told me he attended Catholic schools his whole life, and whenever a priest walked into the room, everyone began to behave better. "You have my permission to be present anywhere, except in the dugout during the game. Major League Baseball does not allow that," he said with a smile.

I had been to spring training in the past to see a couple Cubs games and to be there for the players. During the 2016 spring training, I ran into Coach Maddon in the locker room.

"Fr. Burke," he said, "do you want to practice with the team tomorrow?"

"Really?" I couldn't believe it! I hadn't played ball in a while, and I was forty-nine years old. Once I confirmed that his offer was serious, I responded quickly, "Of course!"

The next day, Joe put me in full uniform and had Miguel Montero, who was with the Cubs at the time and had been coming to Mass, take me out on the field.

"Just go have fun!" were Joe's last instructions to me.

I went out on the practice field with all the players gathered in a circle. After warmups, the players went to different fields, and Miguel invited me to go with him. On this beautiful Arizona spring day, I was on the baseball field again, this time with big leaguers. I didn't realize until I looked around that I was on the field with the entire starting lineup of the Cubs: Rizzo, Bryant, Russell, Heyward, Zobrist, Schwarber, Soler, and Montero. I could see fans asking who I was, and even the players looked at me a little confused. No one recognized me in uniform. Only Miguel knew it was me on the field. We started a drill on baserunning, and I got in the back of the line.

Addison Russell turned around and shook my hand.

"Hi, I'm Addison," he said.

I smiled, shaking his hand.

"Hi, I'm Burke."

The ruse lasted until we were running around the bases and Miguel called out, "Way to go, Father!" After that the players started catching on to who the new "rookie" was.

Once they started hitting, I went to the outfield. I was talking to the pitcher Kyle Hendricks, watching everything on the field, and catching balls. Tears welled up in my eyes. My first thought was, "There is no crying in baseball." Why was I crying? This was a great day, wasn't it? A wave of peace and joy swept over me. It was God's way of saying, "This was your dream: to be a Major League Baseball player. Now you're living my dream of being a priest, and you get to do it in the Major Leagues." It was as though he brought me back to that night before ordination when I asked what was in it for me. This is what he planned all along. This is why he asked me to trust him.

* * *

After that day on the field, a lot of doors opened for me with different guys on the team. When they saw that I could play baseball, I became more relatable for them. Not only was God allowing me to be a part of the major leagues, but he was also blessing my ministry with the guys. Any sacrifice that we make for the Lord, he's going to bless it abundantly.

The Cubs had a great season that year, making it all the way to the National League Championship Series. It was a best-of-seven playoff series to determine who went on to the World Series against the Cleveland Indians. At their Saturday night game against the Los Angeles Dodgers, Miguel hit a grand slam, and the Cubs went on to win. The next morning, Miguel came to Mass in the stands and sat next to popcorn salesmen, beer vendors, and other "regular people." It was beautiful because in God's eyes we're all the same. He doesn't care that Miguel's making millions of dollars and the beer salesmen are making minimum wage. We're all God's children.

I celebrated Mass before the gates opened, but the media saw Miguel come to Mass and surged around us, taking pictures. I felt bad for Miguel because when he came up for Communion, he was swarmed by cameras. Afterward, I apologized to him, but he said that it was okay; he was used to the media attention. The pictures ended up in a lot of newspaper and magazine articles. It brought attention to the fact that there's Mass not only at Wrigley Field but all around Major League Baseball through the Catholic Athletes for

Christ. The next time we had Mass at Wrigley, the Cubs had made it to the World Series, and many more people attended.

The Indians had a 3-1 series lead on the Cubs going into Game 5 of the World Series, which was on a Sunday at Wrigley. It was looking pretty bleak for the Cubs. They had to win the last three games to win the series. That morning at Mass, we had over seventy people in the stands, most likely praying for a miracle. The Cubs beat the Indians 3-2 that day, which meant they were still alive. I didn't travel to Cleveland for Game 6, but that morning, as I was driving up to Mundelein to visit our seminarians, my secretary called.

"It's ESPN," she said. "They called, and they want to interview you tonight before the game."

I thought someone had pulled a prank on me. It was probably Fr. Dennis calling pretending to be ESPN.

"No, Father," she reassured me, "it's really them. Here's their number. I think you should call them."

I called, and much to my surprise, it *was* ESPN. They told me they'd be at the Cubby Bear, a bar right across from Wrigley Field. They wanted me to come down for an interview a few hours before the game. I didn't know what they wanted to talk about, but it would be fun to find out. When I got there, they hooked me up with a microphone. The bar was loud with everyone right behind us drinking and getting ready for Game 6. Just before we went on air, the interviewer was talking to his producer in his earbuds and laughed.

"Father, they want to know if you will give a blessing to the Cubs on the air."

They were joking about the "Curse of the Billy Goat" placed on the Cubs in 1945, when William "Billy Goat" Slanis tried to bring a goat into Wrigley Field on October 6 for Game 4 of the World Series between the Cubs and Detroit Tigers. They did not allow the goat, and Slanis supposedly put a curse on the Cubs. They lost that game and the World Series that year. The Cubs hadn't won a World Series since 1908. Many people throughout the years had tried unsuccessfully to break the curse and end the 108-year losing streak.

I told them I would give a blessing, and the guys behind the camera began counting down, "Five, four, three . . ." I wasn't going to make light of a blessing. After we went on air and talked for a little bit, I prayed that the Cubs play to the best of their ability and that nobody would get hurt. I didn't pray that the Cubs would win because one, I don't think that God cares who wins, and two, there were probably a lot of Indians fans who also prayed that their team would win. At the end of the interview, the interviewer asked if I would come back again the next night if the Cubs won. I accepted his offer.

The Cubs won Game 6, tying the series 3–3. It would all come down to Game 7. That night, I went back to the bar, this time wearing my Cubs practice jersey, the one they gave me at spring training, over my priestly blacks. My white collar stood tall above the blue and red.

"Now, I'm not saying because you prayed, they won," the interviewer said. "But you prayed, and they won. So will you give them another blessing?"

"Sure," I said, and I began praying. This time the bar was quiet behind us. Some people even removed their hats and bowed their heads.

After the interview, I raced out of the city, which was packed. I knew that no matter the outcome of the game, the city was going to get crazy that night. I drove to my friend Joe O'Donnell's house instead, and we all watched in awe as the Cubs led 6–3 by the sixth inning. Many were celebrating, but I and a lot of Cubs fans had a feeling that the game wasn't over. Sure enough, Cleveland came back and tied it 6–6 in the eighth. You could almost hear the collective sigh throughout Chicago. Here we go again! All this way for a loss. Neither team scored in the ninth inning. Then the rain delay hit.

I had 6:30 a.m. Mass the next morning, and figured the delay would last at least thirty minutes, which was how long it would take me to get home. Of course, it was only an eighteen-minute rain delay, and I was driving home when play resumed. I almost drove off the road when I heard the Cubs score two runs in the top of the tenth. Luckily, I got home in time to watch them win it 8–7 in the bottom of the inning. I was by myself jumping up and down in my living room, blown away with gratitude. The Cubs had gone more than a century without winning the World Series—the longest dry spell in Major League history. And God had allowed me to be a small part of it.

The Cubs' management invited everyone, from the players down to the ushers, to take part in the victory parade through Chicago. I am not a huge fan of crowds, and honestly, I didn't expect that I could even make it downtown with the traffic. I just watched the parade from home. I didn't get a World Series ring from the Cubs; they gave them to paid employees, and I'm a volunteer. But that Christmas, one of the seminarians gave me a fake ring he had found online that looks and feels real. I use this ring as a part of my talks to school kids because many ask me if I got a ring from the Cubs. I pull this ring out of my pocket, and they all get excited and applaud.

"You know, this ring is only worth fifteen dollars," I tell them. "I also received a ring for winning the SEC when I was in college. It's a beautiful ring, but now it's in a drawer at home collecting dust. Would it be great to get a ring from the Cubs? Sure, it would. But that ring, too, would end up in a drawer collecting dust. What I want is available to all of us. It never collects dust. No one can steal it from us. It is called the crown of eternal glory."

* * *

I've always had a lot of ambition. I wanted to do something great and make an impact on the world. At first, I thought that would be in sports. I was going to be the best. I was going to change baseball forever! After I became a priest, I thought that maybe that type of ambition was prideful and selfish. I asked my spiritual director once, "Is it okay to have ambition in the spiritual life?" He responded, "As long as the ambition is directed toward God, you can use it for great things. A lot of the saints had great ambition, and they directed all their gifts, talents, and energy toward God. Once you start using your gifts for your glory, be careful. That's when the evil one is involved." This has impacted me greatly, so now I consciously try to use my God-given gifts and talents only for *his* honor and glory.

I had asked God what I would get out of the priesthood the night before ordination, but I don't worry about what I will receive any longer. My focus now is to give honor and glory to God by everything that I think, say, and do. I could not have imagined celebrating the marriage of my friends, participating in the Catholic Baseball Camps, or joining the Cubs organization. I offered everything that I loved to God and said, "Do with them as you will." God took my dreams, purified them, and made them even greater than I could have imagined. He has blessed me in so many ways, and I want to use everything he has given me to honor him and help others get to know his love, mercy, compassion, and generosity.

Our life is not defined by one single moment or by one generous act. Life is not one grand slam, surrounded by a bunch of forgettable moments. Every moment that we are given is an opportunity for a grand slam for God. If you offer your life, your gifts, your talents, and your time to him, there is no telling what your story will be.

QUESTIONS FOR REFLECTION AND DISCUSSION

CHAPTER ONE: A PERFECT GAME PLAN

1. What do you think helped Fr. Burke deal with his not being raised in a religious home?
2. Who are the people in your life who have pushed you to be better and improve, personally and spiritually?
3. Can you point to a specific moment or period of time when your relationship with God began?
4. Where do your identity and worth come from?

CHAPTER TWO: MEETING JESUS

1. A number of factors contributed to Fr. Burke becoming Catholic. What were they and how did they influence his decision?
2. How often do you read the Bible? Has the Bible had a large impact on your faith?
3. Fr. Burke speaks of an ongoing struggle with perfectionism. Do you struggle with wanting to be perfect? How can you open your heart to accept God and his love amid your imperfections?
4. How important is your Baptism to you? Do you celebrate your Baptism like you celebrate your birthday?

CHAPTER THREE: A CHANGE OF PLANS

1. What spiritual perspective did Fr. Burke learn from his baseball failures?
2. How well do you know the content of your faith? Would you be able to explain it to a non-Catholic or non-Christian?
3. God's forgiveness is a free gift. Is it difficult to accept that gift? Are you ever tempted to believe that your sins are too big for God?
4. Our biggest life goals often do not line up with God's will. How willing are you to accept a change of plans if that's what God asks from you?

CHAPTER FOUR: A DIVIDED HEART

1. What experiences and events involving Eucharistic Adoration influenced Fr. Burke's life direction?
2. How attentive to God's will are you? How often do you intentionally pray those words from the Our Father, "Thy will be done"?
3. Reflect on where you are spiritually. What can you do to go deeper? Have you considered going to daily Mass and/or making a regular confession? When is the last time you made a retreat?
4. Do you pray about your vocation? If you are a young person, how seriously have you considered all of the options, including priesthood and the religious life?

CHAPTER FIVE: THE GIFT OF THE RED BIRD

1. Several factors gave Fr. Burke confidence about his priestly vocation. What were they? Why did they have such an impact on him?
2. For Fr. Burke, the cardinal appeared in the yard at the time when he needed it most. Where have you encountered God's presence and love?
3. Have you ever had a crisis of faith? What gave you confidence and courage in that time?
4. Jesus is the source of all healing. Have you gone to him with your wounds?

CHAPTER SIX: FATHER WHAT-A-WASTE!

1. Fr. Burke says that celibacy can bring "real intimacy" and that "the world needs celibacy." What does he mean?
2. "Life is not about material things," Fr. Burke writes, "but about relationships with God and others." Have you prioritized material things over love of God and love of neighbor?
3. What is the ministry of presence? Where can you practice it in your life?
4. Peace comes with following God's will. Have you ever experienced that peace? Is there something God is directing you toward that you are resisting?

CHAPTER SEVEN: A FRIEND OF JESÚS

1. How did Fr. Burke resolve his differences with his pastor? If there is someone in your family or community with whom you sharply disagree, how can you become more unified with them in a similar way?
2. Confronting a difficult incident at his first parish assignment, Fr. Burke thinks, "They didn't prepare me for this in seminary." What unexpected new challenge are you facing right now? How can you rely on God to help see you through?
3. Ministry always involves people with different backgrounds, opinions, and attitudes. Have you ever worked with others in a ministry? What was that experience like? How did you resolve any differences in order to work together?
4. Does a love of neighbor flow from your love of God? Why or why not?

CHAPTER EIGHT: LIVING IN THE MOMENT

1. What did Fr. Burke learn from the experience of two young women who told him that they were in love with him?
2. Fr. Burke learned that loving one's neighbor is not an abstract concept; it really involves paying attention and being kind to the people around you. In what ways can you be more fully present to your neighbor?
3. Have you had a personal encounter with Jesus on a retreat or in the sacraments? What impact did that experience have on your life?
4. Before anointing Irasema, Fr. Burke admits that he wrestled with doubt in the face of dire circumstances. Do you trust that God is working through the sacraments? How can you strengthen that trust?

CHAPTER NINE: SEARCHING FOR MY IDENTITY

1. How did Fr. Burke persuade parents who opposed their sons' vocations to change their mind? How did he support the parents of sons who had entered the seminary?
2. What is your fundamental identity? How do you think God sees you?
3. It is easy to confuse a vocation with a career. How are they different? Do you prioritize one over the other? Why?
4. Do you struggle with thinking that you have to earn God's love?

CHAPTER TEN: A GRAND SLAM FOR GOD

1. How did Fr. Burke use his ambition for greatness as a priest? And how did God bring baseball back into his life?
2. "The measure you give will be the measure you get back" (Luke 6:38). Have you ever experienced this when trying to follow God's will?
3. Many good works in the Church start out as no bigger than a mustard seed. But Jesus says that if we have faith just that big, we can move mountains (Matt. 17:20). Do you trust that God will bring success in what he calls you to do?
4. Do you seek God's honor and glory above all things?